Practice and Skills
Fluency Workbook

Printed in the U.S.A.

ISBN 978-0-544-81747-0
2 3 4 5 6 7 8 9 10   0982   25 24 23 22 21 20 19 18 17
4500694912   B C D E F G

Contents

Student Worksheets

Name _____ Date _____ Class_____

 LESSON 1-1

Precision and Significant Digits

Practice and Problem Solving: A/B

Choose the more precise measurement in each pair.

1. 18 ft; 8 in.   2. 5.8 L; 3 mL   3. 8 pt; 1 gal

_____   _____   _____

4. 7.5 mg; 7.05 mg   5. 67 mm; 4.25 cm   6. 11 oz; 11 lb

_____   _____   _____

Determine the number of significant digits in each measurement.

7. 52.9 km   8. 800 ft   9. 70.09 in.

_____   _____   _____

10. 0.6 mi   11. 23.0 g   12. 3120.58 m

_____   _____   _____

Order each list of units from most precise to least precise.

13. yard, inch, foot, mile   14. gram, centigram, kilogram, milligram

_____   _____

Rewrite each number with the number of significant digits indicated in parentheses.

15. 12.32 lb (2)   16. 1.8 m (1)   17. 34 mi (4)

_____   _____   _____

Solve.

18. A rectangular garden has length of 24 m and width of 17.2 m. Use the correct number of significant digits to write the perimeter of the field.

_____

19. The label on a can of corn indicates a net weight of 14 oz. If the measurement is correct, what is the least that the net weight could be?

_____

20. When two people each measured a window's width, their results were 79 cm and 786 mm. Are these results equally precise? Explain.

_____

_____

Precision and Significant Digits
Reteach

In measurements with different units and the same number of significant digits, the more precise measurement is the one with smaller units.

> Seconds are more precise than hours.
> Feet are more precise than miles.

If the units are the same, the more precise measurement has **more significant digits**.

Examples

Choose the more precise measurement in each pair.

3 ft; 36 in.	An inch is smaller than a foot. 36 inches is more precise.
5 lb; 81 oz	An ounce is smaller than a pound. 81 ounces is more precise.
0.68 c; 0.680 c	0.680 cups is more precise. (3 significant digits)
2450 h; 2405 h	2405 hours is more precise. (4 significant digits)

Choose the more precise measurement in each pair.

1. 5 h; 300 min   2. 3.2 kg; 7.65 g   3. 2.5 in.; 2.50 in.   4. 0.08 qt; 7.203 qt

_____   _____   _____   _____

When calculating with measurements, the answer can be only as precise as the *least* precise measurement.

> When you are **adding or subtracting,**
>   find the number with the fewest decimal places.
>   Round your answer to match.

> When you are **multiplying or dividing,**
>   find the least precise number and count its significant digits.
>   Round your answer to the same number of significant digits.

Examples

Use the correct number of significant digits to rewrite the answer.

2.5 ft × 3.01 ft = 7.525 ft^2	Two significant digits: the answer is 7.5 ft^2.
2.5 ft + 3.01 ft = 5.51 ft	One decimal place: the answer is 5.5 ft.
2.5 ft ÷ 3.01 ft = 0.830565 ft	Two significant digits: the answer is 0.83 ft.

Use the correct number of significant digits to write the answer.

5. 12.8 c ÷ 4 c   6. 30.27 yd + 5.1 yd   7. 9.08 oz − 4.2 oz   8. 6.05 mi × 7 mi

_____   _____   _____   _____

LESSON 1-2

Dimensional Analysis
Practice and Problem Solving: A/B

Determine the conversion factor needed for each conversion.

1. yards into inches

   _____

2. kilograms into pounds mass

   _____

Use dimensional analysis to make each conversion. Write your answer with the correct number of significant digits.

3. 18 feet into meters

   _____

4. 7 centimeters into inches

   _____

5. 2.54 kilograms into pounds

   _____

6. 82 liters into gallons

   _____

Solve. Write your answer with the correct number of significant digits.

7. A car is traveling at 55 miles per hour. Use dimensional analysis to convert the car's speed to feet per minute.

   _____

8. The area of a lot is 12,000 square feet. What is the area in square meters?

   _____

9. A company pays $3.91 million to air a 30-second commercial during a football game that is watched by approximately 115 million potential customers. Calculate the cost per second and the cost per potential customer for this commercial.

   _____

10. A cross-country runner covers 2.5 miles in 12.5 minutes. What is the runner's average speed in miles per hour?

    _____

11. Carpet costs $20 per square yard. How much would it cost to carpet a room measuring 15 feet × 24 feet?

    _____

12. A car averages 32 miles per gallon of gasoline. How far can this car travel on one fluid ounce of gasoline?

    _____

LESSON 1-2

Dimensional Analysis

Reteach

To convert one unit to another, you can use dimensional analysis. You will need the conversion fact that relates the two units.

Convert 10 pints to gallons.

1. Write a conversion fact that relates pints to gallons: 1 gallon is 8 pints.

2. Write the conversion fact as a fraction that equals one. $\frac{1\,gal}{8\,pt} = 1$ or $\frac{8\,pt}{1\,gal} = 1$

3. Use a ? to write an equation for what you want to know. 10 pt = ? gal

4. Multiply 10 pints by the fraction that will cancel pints and leave gallons.

$$\frac{10\;pints}{1} \times \frac{1\,gal}{8\;pints} = \frac{10}{8}\,gal \qquad \text{Reduce to } \frac{5}{4} \text{ or } 1.25 \text{ gallons.}$$

Example

Use dimensional analysis to convert the indicated units. 1 meter is 1.09 yards.

$$5\,m = \underline{\quad}\,yd \qquad 5\,m = ?\,yd; \quad 5\,m \times \frac{1.09\,yd}{1\,m} = 5.45\,yd; \qquad 5\,m = \underline{5.45}\,yd$$

Use dimensional analysis to convert the indicated units.

1. 4 yd = ___ in.   2. 3 pt = ___ gal   3. 15 in. = ___ yd   4. 2 m = ___ yd

5. 14 pt = ___ gal   6. 2 yd = ___ m   7. 5 gal = ___ pt   8. 0.6 yd = ___ in.

To convert an area in square units, multiply by the conversion fraction two times.

$$10\,in^2 = \underline{\quad}\,ft^2 \quad \text{The conversion fraction is } \frac{1\,ft}{12\,in.}.$$

$$\frac{10\;in^2}{1} \times \frac{1\,ft}{12\;in.} \times \frac{1\,ft}{12\;in.} = \frac{10 \times ft \times ft}{12 \times 12} = \frac{10}{144}\,ft^2 \text{ or } 0.07\,ft^2$$

Examples

$$3\,ft^2 = \underline{\quad}\,in^2 \qquad \frac{3\;ft^2}{1} \times \frac{12\,in.}{1\;ft} \times \frac{12\,in.}{1\;ft} = \frac{3 \times 12\,in. \times 12\,in.}{1} = 432\,in^2$$

$$5\,lb/ft = \underline{\quad}\,kg/m \qquad \frac{5\;lb}{1\;ft} \times \frac{1\,kg}{2.2\;lb} \times \frac{1\;ft}{0.3\,m} = \frac{5\,kg}{2.2 \times 0.3\,m} = 7.6\,kg/m$$

Use dimensional analysis to convert the indicated units.

9. 40 in^2 = _____ ft^2 10. 2 mph = _____ ft/min   11. 3 lb/ft = _____ kg/m

Radicals and Rational Exponents
Practice and Problem Solving: A/B

Write the name of the property that is demonstrated by each equation.

1. $(2a)^4 = 16a^4$

2. $(3^6)^3 = 3^{18}$

_____   _____

Simplify each expression.

3. $8^{\frac{2}{3}}$

4. $1^{\frac{3}{5}}$

5. $9^{\frac{1}{2}}$

_____   _____   _____

6. $25^{\frac{3}{2}}$

7. $16^{\frac{5}{4}}$

8. $27^{\frac{1}{3}}$

_____   _____   _____

9. $81^{\frac{1}{4}} + 4^{\frac{1}{2}}$

10. $343^{\frac{2}{3}} \cdot 32^{\frac{2}{5}}$

11. $100^{-\frac{1}{2}}$

_____   _____   _____

Find the value of the expression for the value indicated.

12. $6a^{\frac{3}{4}}$ for $a = 16$

13. $c^{\frac{1}{2}} + c^{\frac{1}{3}}$ for $c = 64$

_____   _____

14. $\dfrac{m^{\frac{3}{5}}}{8}$ for $m = 32$

15. $0.5d^{\frac{5}{7}}$ for $d = 128$

_____   _____

Solve.

16. The equation $t = 0.25d^{\frac{1}{2}}$ can be used to find the number of seconds, t, that it takes an object to fall a distance of d feet. How long does it take an object to fall 64 feet?

_____

17. Show that $\left(16^{\frac{1}{4}}\right)^3$ and $\left(16^3\right)^{\frac{1}{4}}$ are equivalent.

_____

18. The surface area, S, of a cube with volume V can be found using the formula $S = 6V^{\frac{2}{3}}$. Find the surface area of a cube whose volume is 125 cubic inches.

_____

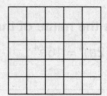

LESSON 2-1   Radicals and Rational Exponents
Reteach

The square checkerboard has 5 units on each side.
Use this to review what you know about exponents and roots.

$$5^2 = 25 \text{ and } \sqrt{25} = 5$$

Notice what happens when you raise a number with an exponent to a power: $(5^2)^3$ means $5^2 \times 5^2 \times 5^2$ or $5 \times 5 \times 5 \times 5 \times 5 \times 5$, which is 5^6. From $(5^2)^3 = 5^6$, you can see that the rule is this:

$$(a^m)^n = a^{mn}.$$

Examples

$$\left(3^3\right)^3 = 3^{3 \cdot 3} = 3^9 = 19{,}683 \qquad \left(2^2\right)^4 = 2^{2 \cdot 4} = 2^8 = 256$$

Squaring and taking the square root undo each other, so $(\sqrt{9})^2 = 9$ because $(3)^2 = 9$.

The rule for square roots is this:

$$\sqrt[2]{y} = y^{\frac{1}{2}}$$

Recall that $\sqrt{y}$ can also be written as $\sqrt[2]{y^1}$.

This is true for all roots.

$$\sqrt[n]{y^m} = y^{\frac{m}{n}}$$ Notice that the index of the $\sqrt{\ }$ is the *bottom*, or denominator, of the fractional exponent.

Examples

$$49^{\frac{1}{2}} = \left(\sqrt[2]{49}\right)^1 = 7 \qquad 1000^{\frac{1}{3}} = \left(\sqrt[3]{1000}\right)^1 = 10 \qquad 16^{\frac{1}{2}} = \left(\sqrt[2]{16}\right)^1 = 4$$

$$8^{\frac{2}{3}} = \left(\sqrt[3]{8}\right)^2 = (2)^2 = 4 \qquad 4^{\frac{5}{2}} = \left(\sqrt[2]{4}\right)^5 = (2)^5 = 32 \qquad 9^{\frac{3}{2}} = \left(\sqrt[2]{9}\right)^3 = (3)^3 = 27$$

Simplify each expression. Show your steps.

1. $100^{\frac{1}{2}}$ 2. $8^{\frac{1}{3}}$ 3. $9^{\frac{1}{2}}$ 4. $25^{\frac{1}{2}}$

_____   _____   _____   _____

5. $4^{\frac{3}{2}}$ 6. $100^{\frac{5}{2}}$ 7. $1000^{\frac{2}{3}}$ 8. $27^{\frac{2}{3}}$

_____   _____   _____   _____

LESSON 2-2

Real Numbers

Practice and Problem Solving: A/B

Write *rational* or *irrational* for each real number.

1. $-\dfrac{2}{3}$

2. 0

3. $\sqrt{11}$

_____

_____

_____

4. $\sqrt[3]{-27}$

5. $\dfrac{\pi}{2}$

6. $\sqrt[5]{5}$

_____

_____

_____

Using *whole*, *integer*, *rational*, and *irrational*, name all of the subsets to which each number belongs.

7. $\dfrac{22}{7}$

8. -19

_____

_____

9. $\sqrt[3]{10}$

10. $\dfrac{32}{8}$

_____

_____

Tell whether the set is closed under the operation indicated. If not closed, provide a counterexample.

11. integers under addition

12. integers under division

_____

_____

13. whole numbers under subtraction

14. Irrational numbers under addition

_____

_____

Solve.

15. Show that the set of non-zero rational numbers is closed under division.

_____

_____

16. Show that the set {−1, 0, 1} is closed under multiplication.

_____

_____

LESSON 2-2

Real Numbers
Reteach

A number line is also called a **Real Number** Line, because every point on the line can be named by a real number and every real number matches a point on the line:

$$\overset{\longleftarrow}{\underset{-3\ -2\ -1\quad 0\quad 1\quad 2\quad 3}{\mid\ \ \mid\ \ \mid\ \ \mid\ \ \mid\ \ \mid\ \ \mid}}\longrightarrow$$

The set of **integers** can be represented by (…, –3, –2, –1, 0, 1, 2, 3, …)

The set of **whole** numbers can be represented by (0, 1, 2, 3, …)

The **ratio** of two integers (such as $\frac{a}{b}$ and $b \neq 0$) is called a **rational** number.

> All integers (7 can be written as $\frac{7}{1}$) and fractions made of integers are rational.

Some real numbers have decimal forms that do *not* repeat or end.

These numbers form the set of **irrational** numbers. Irrational numbers *cannot* be written as the ratio of two integers. Numbers such as $\sqrt{2}, \sqrt{3}, \sqrt{5}, -\sqrt{7},$ and π are irrational numbers. These numbers are real numbers, because they name a point that is on the real number line.

Example

Underline the words that describe this number: $-\frac{2}{3}$

<u>real</u> whole integer positive <u>negative</u> <u>rational</u> irrational

---

Underline the words that describe the number 0.75.

1. real whole integer positive negative irrational rational

When you add two whole numbers, the sum is always a whole number. This means that the set of whole numbers is **closed** under addition. When you subtract two whole numbers, you may get a number that is *not* a whole number. This means that the set of whole numbers is *not* closed under subtraction.

> A set is **closed under an operation** (addition, subtraction, multiplication, division, squaring, taking the square root) ONLY if doing that operation with numbers in the set ALWAYS gives an answer that is in the same set.

Example
Are irrational numbers closed under addition? No, because $\pi + (-\pi) = 0$ which is rational.

Show whether the set is closed under addition using the given numbers.

2. integers; –2 and 4

_____

LESSON 3-1 Evaluating Expressions
Practice and Problem Solving: A/B

Identify the terms and coefficients in each expression.

1. $4a + 6b^2$

2. $x^2 - 9y^2 + 3k$

_____ _____

Evaluate each expression for $n = 6$.

3. $3n - 3$

4. $3(n - 3)$

5. $3n^2 - 3$

_____ _____ _____

Evaluate each expression for $x = 4$ and $y = -2$.

6. $x^2 - y^2$

7. $(x - y)^2$

8. $\dfrac{x}{y} - \dfrac{y}{x}$

_____ _____ _____

Evaluate each expression for $a = 1$, $b = 2$, and $c = -3$.

9. $ab - c$

10. $6abc^2 + 6a^2bc$

11. $(a + b + c)^{10} - abc$

_____ _____ _____

Solve.

12. The expression $\dfrac{D}{t}$ can be used to find a car's average speed, where

    D = distance traveled and t = time spent traveling. Find the average
    speed of a car that travels 240 miles in 5 hours.

    _____

13. The expression $1.8C + 32$ can be used to convert C, any Celsius
    temperature, into its corresponding Fahrenheit temperature. What
    Fahrenheit temperature corresponds to $-10°$ Celsius?

    _____

14. A cell phone plan costs $30 per month and includes 400 free minutes.
    Additional minutes then cost $0.15 apiece. If a subscriber uses more
    than 400 minutes, the cost, in dollars, can be found using the
    expression $30 + 0.15(m - 400)$, where m represents the total number
    of minutes used. Find the cost for a month in which a subscriber used
    525 minutes.

    _____

LESSON 3-1 Evaluating Expressions

Reteach

The **terms** in an algebraic expression are separated by + or − signs.

$3x + 5$ has two terms.

$3(x + 5)$ has just one term. (Three is multiplied by the contents of the parentheses.)

$7x + 3y − 5$ has three terms.

$4(x − 2) − y$ has two terms. The first term is $4(x − 2)$ and $−y$ is the second term.

In the expression $8 + 4x − 3x^2$, 8 is a **constant** or an unchanging stand-alone number.
The multipliers 4 and −3 are **coefficients,** and 2 is an **exponent**.

Examples

Use this expression:	$9 − 5x − 6x^3$.
Write the terms.	$9, − 5x, −6x^3$
Write the constant term.	9
Write the coefficients.	−5 and −6
Write the exponent.	2

Evaluate an algebraic expression by substituting the given value for the variable.

To simplify the results, use the order of operations.

First, simplify inside parentheses.

Second, simplify any expression with an exponent.

Third, do the multiplication and division in order from left to right.

Finally, do the addition and subtraction in order from left to right.

Examples

Evaluate $7 + 3b$ for $b = 2$.

$7 + 3(2)$	Substitute the value 2 for b in the expression.
$7 + 6 = 13$	Multiply 3 times 2 before adding the product to 7.

Evaluate $8x − 7x + 2x$ for $x = 3$.

$8(3) − 7(3) + 2(3)$	Substitute the value 3 for the variable x.
$24 − 21 + 6$	Multiply in order from left to right.
$3 + 6 = 9$	Add and subtract in order from left to right.

Evaluate each expression for $x = −3$, $y = 2$, and $z = 5$.

1. $10 − 4y$

2. $y^2(x + 16)$

3. $3x − 5y + 8$

4. $z + 3y − x^2$

5. $7y^2 + xz$

6. $(z − x)(x + 7)$

7. $9 − 3(y − z)^2$

8. $(y + z) − yz$

9. $z + (y − x)^2$

LESSON 3-2

Simplifying Expressions
Practice and Problem Solving: A/B

Identify each property illustrated.

1. $6x + 7 = 7 + 6x$

    _____

2. $8(m - 6) = 8m - 48$

    _____

3. $y + (3 + 2y) = y + (2y + 3)$

    _____

4. $(2k)(w) = (2)(kw)$

    _____

Simplify each expression.

5. $12x - 7 + 3x$

    _____

6. $8k + 3k - 9k$

    _____

7. $2(a + 4) + 11$

    _____

8. $9w - 3 + 2w - 7$

    _____

9. $x + 5(2x - 3) + 3$

    _____

10. $-5m - 2m$

    _____

11. $(x + y) + 4(2x - y)$

    _____

12. $3(a + b) - 3(a - b)$

    _____

13. $100 - 7(3x - 4) + 10x$

    _____

14. $-8 + 2(8 - 2x) + 11x$

    _____

15. $16z - 3(5z + c) + 2c$

    _____

16. $19 + 4n - 10(t - n)$

    _____

Solve.

17. Kitchen goods are on sale for 30% off their regular price. In addition,
    all goods are subject to 6% tax and a $6 shipping charge. If c
    represents the original cost of a blender, its total cost can be found
    using the expression $1.06(0.7c) + 6$. Find the total cost of a blender
    that originally cost $65.

    _____

18. In Problem 17, explain where the coefficient 0.7 comes from.

    _____

Simplifying Expressions

**LESSON
3-2**

Reteach

$7x + 3x$ can be rewritten as $10x$. This is called *simplifying*.

The value stays the same when you simplify, so the two expressions are **equivalent**.

To simplify, use the properties of numbers.

> The Commutative Property says you can add or multiply in any order.
> $$3a + 2b = 2b + 3a \qquad \text{and} \qquad 4xy = 4yx$$

> The Associative Property says you can add or multiply with different groups.
> $$(11 + 3a) + 2a = 11 + (3a + 2a)$$

> The Distributive Property says you can multiply using parentheses.
> $$5(2a - 3) = 5(2a) - 5(3) = 10a - 15$$

Example

Name the property that shows the two expressions are equivalent.

$3r + 7r = r(3 + 7)$	Distributive Property
$r(3 + 7) = (3 + 7)r$	Commutative Property of Multiplication
$(4 + 3r) + 2r = 4 + (3r + 2r)$	Associative Property of Addition

---

To simplify an expression, use the properties and combine like terms.
Like terms have the same variable with the same exponent.

Examples

7 and 9 are like terms. Both are constants with no variable. Combine to 16.
$3k$ and $7k$ are like terms. Combine to $10k$.
$2y^2$ and $-5y^2$ are like terms. Combine to $-3y^2$.
$6y$ and 3 are NOT like terms. They cannot be combined.
$4y$ and $3x$ are NOT like terms. They cannot be combined.
$8y^2$ and $3y$ are NOT like terms. They cannot be combined.
$3x + 2(5 + 4x)$ can be simplified to $3x + 10 + 8x$ which is $11x + 10$.

Simplify each expression.

1. $7b - 3b$

2. $3x + 8y + 9x$

3. $6(x^2 + 1) + 2x$

4. $-2(x - 1) + 7x + 4$

5. $2 + 3(x + 5) - x$

6. $7(x^2 + 2) + 3x^2$

Name the property used.

7. $(3x + 8y) + 5x =$
   $3x + (8y + 5x)$

8. $3x + 8y + 5x =$
   $3x + 5x + 8y$

9. $2(3x - 5) = 6x - 10$

LESSON 3-3

Writing Expressions

Practice and Problem Solving: A/B

Write each expression using *n* as your variable. Then simplify fully.

1. Five more than the sum of a number and ten

   _____

2. The product of eight and seven less than a number

   _____

3. The quotient of a number and three, increased by one

   _____

4. Ten less than the product of six and eight less than a number

   _____

5. The difference of one less than a number and twice the number

   _____

6. A number times its opposite, increased by seven

   _____

Solve.

7. Eliza earns $400 per week plus $15 for each new customer she signs
   up. Let *c* represent the number of new customers Eliza signs up. Write
   an expression that shows how much she earns in a week. Then find
   how much Eliza earns in a week in which she signs up 18 customers.

   _____

8. Max's car holds 18 gallons of gasoline. Driving on the highway, the car
   uses approximately 2 gallons per hour. Let *h* represent the number of
   hours Max has been riding on the highway. Write an expression that
   shows how many gallons of gasoline Max has left after driving *h* hours.
   Then find that number after Max drives 3.5 hours on the highway.

   _____

9. A man's age today is three years less than four times the age of his
   oldest daughter. Let *a* represent the daughter's age. Write an
   expression to represent the man's age. Then find his age if the oldest
   daughter is 11 years old.

   _____

LESSON 3-3 Writing Expressions
Reteach

To translate words into expressions, find words like these that tell you the operation.

+	−	•	÷
add	subtract	multiply	divide
sum	difference	product	quotient
more	less	times	split
increased	decreased	per	ratio

Examples

Three more than 5 times the sum of Ken's DVDs and 4 is equal to Martin's DVDs.

$$3 + 5 \cdot (k + 4) = m$$
$$3 + 5k + 20 = m$$
$$5k + 23 = m$$

Use the words to write the equation, then simplify.

If Ken has 6 DVDs, how many does Martin have?.

Substitute 6 for k and simplify.

$$m = 5k + 23$$
$$m = 5(6) + 23$$
$$m = 30 + 23$$
$$m = 53; \text{ Martin has 53 DVDs.}$$

Mrs. Knight drives to the train station for half an hour at 30 miles per hour, and then walks 0.75 miles to her office. What is the total distance she travels?

$$\left(0.5 \text{ hr} \times \frac{30 \text{mi}}{\text{hr}} \right) + 0.75 \text{ mi}$$

15 mi + 0.75 mi
She travels 15.75 miles in all.

Write an expression. Simplify if possible.

1. Enrique collected 7 more than 2 times as many recyclable bottles as Natasha. Write an expression for the number of bottles they collected altogether.

_____

2. Mr. McKay spent $2.60 for a box of crackers and then divided them evenly between the s students in his classroom. Write an expression for the cost of crackers for each student.
   Find the cost for $s = 20$ students.

_____

3. Jean walked 1 mile to her friend's house, and then bicycled for 2 hours at 5 miles per hour. Write an expression for the total length of her trip, and find the length of the trip.

_____

Equations in One Variable

Practice and Problem Solving: A/B

Solve each equation.

1. $4t + 13 = 5$
        2. $6.3 = 2x - 4.5$
        3. $12 = -r - 11$

_____   _____   _____

4. $-5y + 6 = -9$
        5. $-1 = \dfrac{b}{4} - 7$
        6. $\dfrac{5}{8} = 2m + \dfrac{3}{8}$

_____   _____   _____

7. $x + -4 + 2x = 14$
        8. $4(y + 1) = -8$
        9. $-2(d + 6) = -10$

_____   _____   _____

10. $2(c + 3) = c - 13$
        11. $5p - 8 = 1 + 5p - 9$
        12. $3(2v - 1) = 6v - 4$

_____   _____   _____

13. $2y + 3 = 3(y + 7)$
        14. $4n + 6 - 2n = 2(n + 3)$
        15. $6m - 8 = 2 + 9m - 1$

_____   _____   _____

16. $-v + 5 + 6v = 1 + 5v + 3$
        17. $2(3b - 4) = 8b - 11$
        18. $5(r - 1) = 2(r - 4) - 6$

_____   _____   _____

Write and solve an equation to solve each problem.

19. When angles are complementary, the sum of their measures is
90 degrees. Two complementary angles have measures of $2x - 10$
degrees and $3x - 10$ degrees. Find the measures of each angle.

_____

20. Jan's age is three years less than twice Tritt's age. The sum of their
ages is 30. Find their ages.

_____

21. Iris charges $50 for her consulting services plus $60 for each hour she works.
On one job, Iris charged $470. For how many hours did Iris work on this job?

_____

22. Three players scored a total of 70 points during a basketball game.
One player scored twice as many as one teammate and ten points fewer
than the other teammate. How many points did each player score?

_____

LESSON 4-1

Equations in One Variable

Reteach

To **solve** an equation, get the variable alone: $x = 3$.

To get the variable alone, or *isolate* the variable, you UNDO what has been done.

$-5 = \underline{x} - 8$ Underline the variable so you know what to isolate.
Ask yourself "What was DONE to this variable? How can I UNDO it?"

In this equation, 8 has been *subtracted from* the variable. How do you UNDO subtraction?

Addition and Subtraction UNDO each other. (These are **inverse** operations.)
Multiplication and Division UNDO each other. (Also **inverse** operations.)

$-5 = \underline{x} - 8$ Keep the equation true by doing the same thing to *both sides.*
$\underline{+8 \qquad +8}$
$\quad 3 = x$ Check by substituting into the original equation. →

$-5 = x - 8$
$-5 \overset{?}{=} 3 - 8$
$-5 = -5 ✓$

Example

$\dfrac{3}{4}y = 9$ UNDO multiplying by a fraction by multiplying by its reciprocal.

$\dfrac{4}{3}\left(\dfrac{3}{4}y\right) = 9\left(\dfrac{4}{3}\right)$ The fractions multiply to 1, and $1y = y$.

$y = 12$ Check: Does $\dfrac{3}{4}(12) = 9$? Yes.

Solve each equation and check.

1. $-8 = x - 2$

2. $x + 4 = 12$

3. $6z = -42$

_____   _____   _____

If the variable is on *both sides* of the equation, collect the variable terms on one side of the equation and the constants on the opposite side. Once the variable term is isolated, you can solve for the variable.

Example

$8 - 5x = 2 - 3x$ First, UNDO the addition and subtraction.
$\underline{-2 + 5x = -2 + 5x}$ Subtract 2 and add 5x on both sides.
$\quad 6 \qquad = \quad 2x$ Last, UNDO the multiplication by 2 by dividing by 2.
$\qquad 3 = x$ Check: Is $8 - 5(3) = 2 - 3(3)$? Yes, because $-7 = -7$.

Solve each equation and check.

4. $3x - 8 = 4$

5. $\dfrac{b}{2} - 4 = 26$

6. $5y + 4 - 2y = 9$

_____   _____   _____

7. $14 = 3(x - 2) + 5$

8. $10x = 2x - 16$

9. $-2x + 8 = 2x + 4$

_____   _____   _____

LESSON 4-2

Inequalities in One Variable
Practice and Problem Solving: A/B

Solve and graph each inequality.

1. $2x \geq 6$

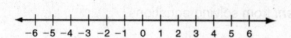

2. $\dfrac{a}{5} < 1$

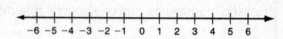

3. $5x + 7 \geq 2$

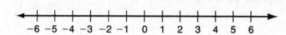

4. $5(z + 6) \leq 40$

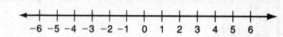

5. $5x \geq 7x + 4$

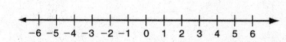

6. $3(b - 5) < -2b$

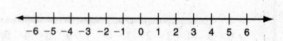

Write and solve an inequality for each problem.

7. By selling old CDs, Sarah has a store credit for $153. A new CD costs $18. What are the possible numbers of new CDs Sarah can buy?

_____

_____

8. Ted needs an average of at least 70 on his three history tests. He has already scored 85 and 60 on two tests. What is the minimum grade Ted needs on his third test?

_____

_____

9. Jay can buy a stereo either online or at a local store. If he buys online, he gets a 15% discount, but has to pay a $12 shipping fee. At the local store, the stereo is not on sale, but there is no shipping fee. For what regular prices is it cheaper for Jay to buy the stereo online?

_____

_____

LESSON 4-2

Inequalities in One Variable

Reteach

An inequality, such as $2x < 8$, has infinitely many numbers in its solution. For example, $2, 0, -\frac{1}{2}$, and -350 are all values of x that make this inequality true.

Solve an inequality by UNDOING what has been done to x, using the same steps as for an equality, with the *exception* given below.

Solving inequalities has one special rule *different* from solving equations.

Multiplying or dividing an inequality by a NEGATIVE number REVERSES the inequality sign.

Show the solution set by graphing on a number line. When you graph a solution, begin with an open circle for $<$ and $>$ and use a closed circle for $\leq$ and $\geq$.

Example

$-3x < 15$ Note that 6 and 8 make this true, but it is *not* true for -6 or -8.

$\dfrac{-3x}{-3} > \dfrac{15}{-3}$ Dividing by -3 REVERSES the inequality sign.

$x > -5$ This is still true for 6 and 8, and not true for -6 or -8.

Solve and graph each inequality.

1. $-3e - 10 \leq -4$

2. $\dfrac{c}{2} + 8 > 11$

3. $15 \leq 3 - 4s$

4. $\dfrac{3}{4}j + 1 > 4$

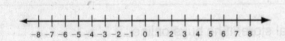

Solve each inequality.

5. $8c + 4 > 4(c - 3)$ 6. $5(x - 1) < 3x + 10 - 8x$ 7. $-8 + 4a - 12 > 2a + 10$

Solving for a Variable
Practice and Problem Solving: A/B

Solve the equation for the indicated variable.

1. $x = 5y$ for y

2. $s + 4t = r$ for s

3. $3m - 7n = p$ for m

_____

_____

_____

4. $6 = hj + k$ for j

5. $\dfrac{v}{w} = 9$ for w

6. $\dfrac{a+3}{b} = c$ for a

_____

_____

_____

Solve the formula for the indicated variable.

7. Formula for the circumference of a circle:

$S = 2\pi r$, for r

8. Formula for the area of a triangle:

$A = \dfrac{1}{2}bh$, for b

_____

_____

9. Formula for the semiperimeter of a triangle:

$s = \dfrac{a + b + c}{2}$, for c

10. Formula for the volume of a cone:

$V = \dfrac{1}{3}\pi r^2 h$, for h

_____

_____

11. Formula for the area of a trapezoid:

$A = \dfrac{1}{2}(a + b)h$, for a

12. Formula for the volume of a cylinder:

$V = \pi r^2 h$, for r

_____

_____

Solve.

13. Janet earns $300 per week plus a commission of 10% on all sales that she makes. Write a formula for E, Janet's weekly earnings, in terms of s, her sales for the week. Then solve your formula for s.

_____

14. A handyman charges a fixed rate of r to visit a customer's house. In addition, the handyman charges an hourly rate of h for each hour worked. Write a formula to represent T, the total amount this handyman would charge for a job that requires n hours of work.

_____

15. Solve your formula from Problem 14 for h. Then find the handyman's hourly rate if his fixed rate is $20 and he charges $200 for a 4-hour job.

_____

LESSON 4-3

Solving for a Variable
Reteach

Solving for a variable in a formula can make it easier to use.
    You can solve a formula, or literal equation, for any one of the variables.

To solve a literal equation or formula, underline the variable you are solving for, and then UNDO what has been done to that variable. Use inverse operations in the same way you do when solving an equation or inequality.

The formula for finding the area of a rectangle when you know length and width is $A = lw$. If you know the area and the length, you could find the width by using a formula for w.

Examples

Solve $A = lw$ for w.   Since w is multiplied by l, use division to undo this.

$$\frac{A}{l} = \frac{lw}{l}$$ Divide both sides by l.

$$\frac{A}{l} = w \text{ or } w = \frac{A}{l}$$

Solve $\frac{y-b}{m} = x$ for b.   What has been done to b? First **undo** dividing by m.

$$(m)\frac{y-b}{m} = x(m)$$ Multiply both sides by m.

$$y - b = xm$$

$$\underline{-y \qquad\qquad -y}$$ Subtract y from both sides.

$$-b = xm - y$$ Finally, multiply both sides by -1 to solve for b.

$$(-1)(-b) = (-1)(xm - y)$$

$$b = -xm + y \text{ or } b = y - xm$$

Solve each formula for the indicated variable.

1. $A = \frac{1}{2}(a+b)h$, for b

2. $d = rt$, for r

3. $P = \frac{3x + 10n + 9}{3}$, for x

_____

4. $P = 2l + 2w$, for w

5. $V = \frac{1}{3}lwh$, for h

6. $P = \frac{KT}{V}$, for K

_____

Solve each equation for the indicated variable.

7. $a + b + c = 180$, for b

8. $x = ay + a$, for y

9. $\frac{m}{n} = \frac{p}{q}$, for m

_____

10. $x = \frac{y-z}{10}$, for y

11. $a = b + \frac{c}{d}$, for c

12. $y = x + \frac{z}{3}$, for x

_____

LESSON 5-1

Equations in Two Variables

Practice and Problem Solving: A/B

For each equation, find the ordered pair whose *x*-coordinate is −4.

1. $y = 18 − 5x$

2. $2x + 3y = 4$

3. $−7x + 6y = 10$

_____   _____   _____

For each equation, find the ordered pairs whose *x*-coordinates are 3 or −3.

4. $x = 2y + 1$

5. $\dfrac{x}{3} − \dfrac{y}{3} = 1$

6. $3x − y + 10 = 0$

_____   _____   _____

For each equation, find *y* for *x* = −2, −1, 0, 1, and 2. List the ordered pairs and then graph the equation on the coordinate grid given.

7. $y = 2x − 3$

8. $x + y = 4$

_____   _____

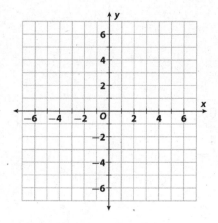   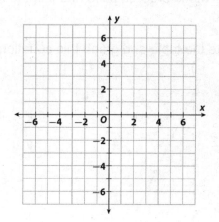

9. $y = −3x + 1$

10. $x − 2y + 10 = 0$

_____   _____

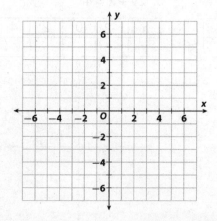   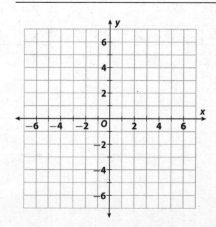

LESSON 5-1

Equations in Two Variables

Reteach

Solutions to equations with two variables, *x* and *y*, are *ordered pairs*.

> An ordered pair is a *solution* to an equation if the equation is true when you *substitute* the first coordinate for *x* and the second coordinate for *y*. For example, the ordered pair (3, 5) is a solution to $x + y = 8$ because $3 + 5 = 8$.

The equation $x + y = 8$ has *infinitely many* solutions, or ordered pairs, that make it true. You can use a table to represent *some* of the ordered pairs in the solution of $x + y = 8$.

x	−1	0	2	4	5	8	9
y	9	8	6	4	3	0	−1

You can picture *all* of the solutions to $x + y = 8$ by drawing the graph of this equation.

The *graph* of an equation contains every pair of points that make the equation true.

To graph an equation, find at least three pairs of values for *x* and *y* that make the equation true. Plot those ordered pairs and join them with a straight line that extends both directions.

Example

Complete the table and graph this equation: $y = 4 - 2x$

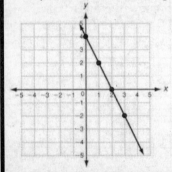

x	3	2	1	0
y	−2	0	2	4

Complete each table and graph each equation.

1. $4y = 3x - 12$

x	−2	0	2	4
y				

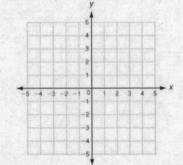

2. $y = x + 3$

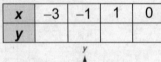

x	−3	−1	1	0
y				

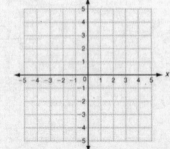

3. $2y + x = 4$

x	−2	0	2	4
y				

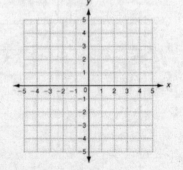

LESSON 5-2

Representing Functions

Practice and Problem Solving: A/B

Express each relation as a table, as a graph, and as a mapping diagram.

1. {(–2, 5), (–1, 1), (3, 1), (–1, –2)}

x	y

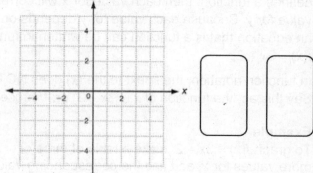

2. {(5, 3), (4, 3), (3, 3), (2, 3), (1, 3)}

x	y

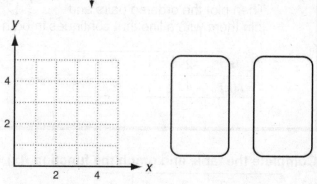

Give the domain and range of each relation. Tell whether the relation is a function. Explain.

3.

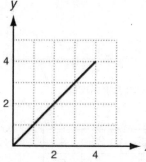

D: _____

R: _____

Function? _____

Explain: _____

_____

_____

_____

4.

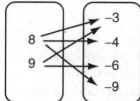

D: _____

R: _____

Function? _____

Explain: _____

_____

_____

_____

5.

x	y
1	4
2	5
0	6
1	7
2	8

D: _____

R: _____

Function? _____

Explain: _____

_____

_____

_____

LESSON 5-2

Representing Functions
Reteach

An equation such as $y = 3x + 2$ defines a **function**. If you choose a value
for x, you can then calculate a corresponding value for y. If the equation
defines a function, then each value for x will correspond with *only one
value for y*. Because each value for y depends on the chosen value for x,
an equation that is a function can be written in function notation, such as
$f(x) = 3x + 2$.

In function notation, the f next to the (x) does NOT mean to multiply.
Say this as "the function of x is $3x + 2$" or, "f of x equals $3x + 2$."

Example
To graph $f(x) = 3x + 2$, make a table of three or
more values for x, and find the corresponding values for y.
　　　Then plot the ordered pairs and
　　　join them with a line that continues in both directions.

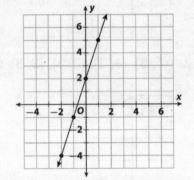

x	−2	−1	0	1
f(x)	−4	−1	2	5

Complete the table and graph the function $f(x) = -2x - 4$.

1.

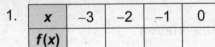

x	−3	−2	−1	0
f(x)				

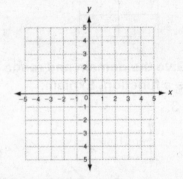

The **domain** of a function is the set of values for **x**.
The **range** of a function is the set of values for **y**.
In the function $f(x) = -2x - 4$, both the domain and the range are all real numbers.

Example
Does this table describe a function? Explain.
　　　If it is a function, give the domain and range.
Yes, because each x is paired with only one y.
The domain is {1, 2, 3, 4}, and the range is {3, 4, 5}.

x	1	2	3	4
f(x)	3	3	4	5

Tell whether each pairing of numbers describes a function.
If so, write the function and give the domain and range.

2.

x	0	1	2	3
f(x)	0	−1	−2	−3

3.

x	0	1	1	4
f(x)	0	1	−1	2

4.

x	0	1	2	3
f(x)	1	2	3	4

_____ 　　 _____ 　　 _____

_____ 　　 _____ 　　 _____

LESSON 5-3

Sequences
Practice and Problem Solving: A/B

Find the first four terms of each sequence.

1. $f(n) = 3n - 1$

2. $f(n) = n^2 + 2n + 5$

3. $f(n) = \dfrac{n+6}{2n+3}$

4. $f(n) = \sqrt{n-1}$

5. $f(n) = (n-1)(n-2)$

6. $f(1) = 3$, $f(n) = f(n-1) + 7$ for $n \geq 2$

7. $f(1) = 9$, $f(n) = 2f(n-1) + 1$ for $n \geq 2$

8. $f(n) = \dfrac{n(n+1)}{2}$

9. $f(1) = 6$, $f(n) = -\dfrac{1}{f(n-1)}$ for $n \geq 2$

10. $f(1) = 16$, $f(n) = \sqrt{f(n-1)}$ for $n \geq 2$

A ferry charges \$40 for each car and \$8.50 for each person in the car.
Use this information for Problems 11–16.

11. Find the cost for a car containing only a driver.

12. Find the cost for a car containing four people.

13. Write an explicit rule for this situation.

14. Write a recursive rule for this situation.

15. A car is charged \$91. Determine how many people are in the car.

16. Explain whether this situation represents a function or not.

Sequences

Reteach

A list of numbers in a specific order, or pattern, is called a **sequence**. Each number, or **term**, in the sequence corresponds with the position number that locates it in the list. For example, in the sequence 2, 4, 6, 8.., the first term is 2, the second term is 4, and the third term is 6.

You can write a sequence as a function, where the domain is {1, 2, 3, 4,...} or the set of position numbers. The range is the set of the numbers, or terms, in the list.

Domain or position number: n	1	2	3	4	5
Range or term: $f(n)$	2	4	6	8	10

This sequence can be described by an **explicit rule** that defines each $f(n)$ in terms of n.

For the table above, the explicit rule is $f(n) = 2n$.
Using this rule, calculate the 11th term ($n = 11$) of this sequence: $f(11) = 2(11)$ or 22.

Example
Complete this table by finding the first 4 terms of the sequence defined by $f(n) = n(n + 1)$.
Then find the 10th term of the sequence.

n	1	2	3	4	...10
$f(n)$	$1(1 + 1) = 2$	$2(2 + 1) = 6$	$3(3 + 1) = 12$	$4(4 + 1) = 20$	$10(10 + 1) = 110$

Complete each table for the given sequence.

1. $f(n) = 3n + 2$

n	1	2	3	4
$f(n)$				

2. $f(n) = \frac{1}{2}n + 1$

n	1	2	3	4
$f(n)$				

3. $f(n) = n - 1$

n	1	2	3	4
$f(n)$				

In a sequence, the term *before* the nth term can be written as $f(n - 1)$. Sometimes a sequence is described by giving the first term, then the rule defines each term *after* the first one by using the term before. A rule that does this is called a **recursive rule**.

Example
Write the first four terms of the sequence with $f(1) = 3$ and $f(n) = f(n - 1) + 5$ for $n \geq 2$.
   3, (3) + 5, (3 + 5) + 5, (3 + 5 + 5) + 5 which simplifies to 3, 8, 13, 18.

Write the first four terms of each sequence.

4. $f(1) = 10$ and $f(n) = f(n - 1) - 2$ for $n \geq 2$

5. $f(1) = -4$ and $f(n) = f(n - 1) + 3$ for $n \geq 2$

_____   _____

LESSON 6-1

Linear Functions
Practice and Problem Solving: A/B

Tell whether each function is linear or not.

1. $y = 3x^2$

2. $7 - y = 5x + 11$

3. $-2(x + y) + 9 = 1$

_____ _____ _____

The standard form of a linear equation is $Ax + By = C$. For each set of values given, tell if the linear equation represents a horizontal line, a vertical line or neither.

4. $A = 2, B = 2, C = 2$

5. $A = 0, B = 5, C = 0$

6. $A = -8, B = 0, C = 8$

_____ _____ _____

Graph each line.

7. $y = \dfrac{1}{2}x - 3$

8. $2x + 3y = 8$

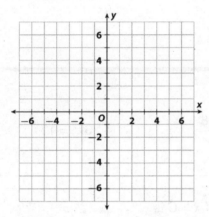   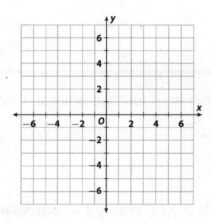

The solid and dashed graphs below show how two consultants charge for their daily services. Use the graphs for Problems 9–11.

9. How much does each charge for a 6-hour job?

_____

10. Does either consultant charge according to a linear function?

_____

11. For which length of job do A and B charge the same amount?

_____

Name _____ Date _____ Class_____

Linear Functions
Reteach

The graph of a **linear function** is a straight line.

$Ax + By + C = 0$ is the **standard form** for the equation of a linear function.

- A, B, and C are real numbers. A and B are not both zero.

- The variables x and y
    - have exponents of 1
    - are not multiplied together
    - are not in denominators, exponents or radical signs.

Examples   **These are NOT linear functions:**

$2 + 4 = 6$	no variable
$x^2 = 9$	exponent on $x \geq 1$
$xy = 8$	x and y multiplied together
$\dfrac{6}{x} = 3$	x in denominator
$2^y = 8$	y in exponent
$\sqrt{y} = 5$	y in a square root

Tell whether each function is linear or not.

1. $14 = 2\sqrt{x}$ 2. $3xy = 27$ 3. $14 = \dfrac{28}{x}$ 4. $6x^2 = 12$

_____ _____ _____ _____

The graph of $y = C$ is always a **horizontal** line. The graph of $x = C$ is always a **vertical** line.

Examples

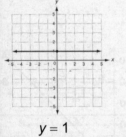
$y = 1$

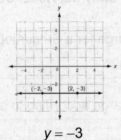
$y = -3$

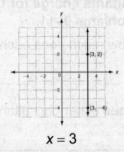
$x = 3$

$x = 2$

Tell whether each equation represents a horizontal line, a vertical line, or neither..

5. $9y = 27$ 6. $6x + 7y = 10$ 7. $\dfrac{1}{2}x = 19$ 8. $x = 0$

_____ _____ _____ _____

LESSON 6-2 **Using Intercepts**

Practice and Problem Solving: A/B

Find each x- and y-intercept.

1.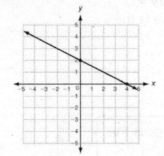

2.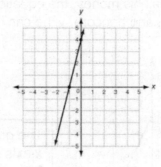

3.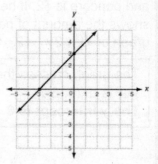

_____   _____   _____

_____   _____   _____

Use intercepts to graph the line described by each equation.

4. $3x + 2y = -6$

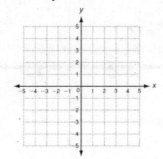

5. $x - 4y = 4$

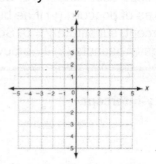

6. At a fair, hamburgers sell for $3.00 each and hot dogs sell for $1.50 each. The equation $3x + 1.5y = 30$ describes the number of hamburgers and hot dogs a family can buy with $30.

   a. Find the intercepts and graph the function.

   _____

   b. What does each intercept represent?

   _____

   _____

   _____

   _____

LESSON 6-2

Using Intercepts
Reteach

Doug has $12 to spend on popcorn and peanuts. The peanuts are $4 and popcorn is $2. If he spends all his money, the equation $4x + 2y = 12$ shows the amount of peanuts, x, and popcorn, y, he can buy. Here is the graph of $4x + 2y = 12$.

The graph crosses the *y*-axis at (0, 6).
The *y*-intercept is 6.

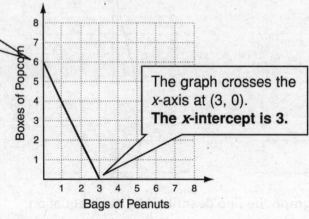

The graph crosses the *x*-axis at (3, 0).
The *x*-intercept is 3.

To find the *y*-intercept, substitute $x = 0$. Solve for *y*. $4(0) + 2y = 12$
He can buy 6 boxes of popcorn (*y*) if he buys 0 peanuts. $y = 6$
To find the *x*-intercept, substitute $y = 0$. Solve for *x*. $4x + 2(0) = 12$
He can buy 3 bags of peanuts (*x*) if he buys 0 popcorn. $x = 3$

Find each *x*- and *y*-intercept.

1.
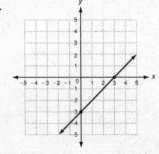

_____

2.
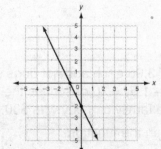

_____

3.
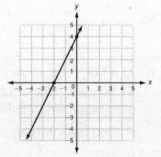

_____

Find each intercept. Use these two points to graph each line.

4. $3x + 9y = 9$
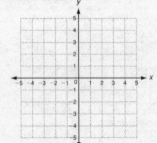

5. $4x + 6y = -12$
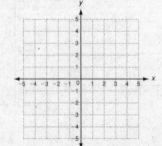

6. $2x - y = 4$
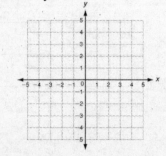

LESSON
6-3

Using Slope

Practice and Problem Solving: A/B

Find the rise and run between the marked points on each graph.
Then find the slope of the line.

1.

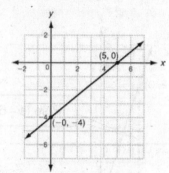

rise = _____ run = _____

slope = _____

2.

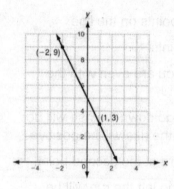

rise = _____ run = _____

slope = _____

3.

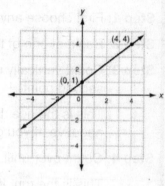

rise = _____ run = _____

slope = _____

Find the slope of each line. Tell what the slope represents.

4.

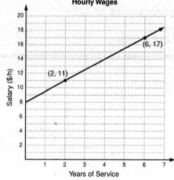

_____

_____

5.

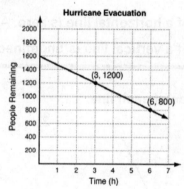

_____

_____

Solve.

6. When ordering tickets online, a college theater charges a $5 handling
   fee no matter how large the order. Tickets to a comedy concert cost
   $58 each. If you had to graph the line showing the total cost, *y*, of
   buying *x* tickets, what would the slope of your line be? Explain your
   thinking.

   _____

   _____

Using Slope
Reteach

Find the rate of change, or **slope**, for the graph of a straight line by finding $\dfrac{\text{change in } y}{\text{change in } x}$.

Step 1: First choose any two points on the line.

Step 2: Begin at one of the points.

Step 3: Count vertically until you are even with the
second point.

    This is the rise. If you go down the rise will be
negative. If you go up the rise will be positive.

Step 4: Count over until you are at the second point.

    This is the run. If you go left the run will be
negative. If you go right the run will be positive.

Step 5: Divide to find the slope.

$$\text{slope} = \dfrac{\text{rise}}{\text{sun}} = -\dfrac{6}{2} = -3$$

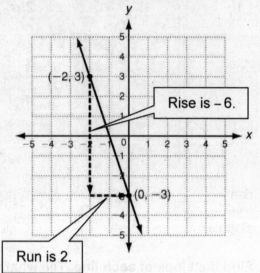

Rise is – 6.

Run is 2.

The **slope of a horizontal line is zero**. A horizontal line has no steepness at all.

The **slope of a vertical line is undefined**. A vertical line is infinitely steep.

Find the slope of each line.

1.
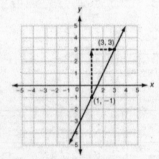

_____

2.
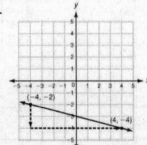

_____

3.
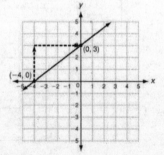

_____

4.
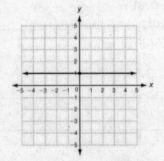

_____

5.
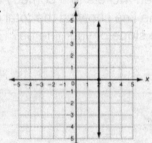

_____

6.
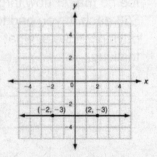

_____

LESSON 6-4

Slope-Intercept Form
Practice and Problem Solving: A/B

Write each line in slope-intercept form. Then identify the slope and the *y*-intercept.

1. $4x + y = 7$

   Equation: _____

   Slope: _____

   y-intercept: _____

2. $2x - 3y = 9$

   Equation: _____

   Slope: _____

   y-intercept: _____

3. $5x + 1 = 4y + 7$

   Equation: _____

   Slope: _____

   y-intercept: _____

4. $3x + 2y = 2x + 8$

   Equation: _____

   Slope: _____

   y-intercept: _____

Graph each function.

5. $f(x) = -3x + 4$

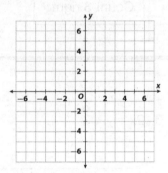

6. $f(x) = \dfrac{5}{6}x - 1$

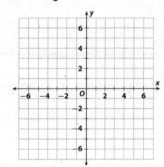

Solve.

7. State the domain and range of the functions from Problems 5 and 6.

   _____

8. A line has *y*-intercept of –11 and slope of 0.25. Write its equation in slope-intercept form.

   _____

9. A tank can hold 30,000 gallons of water. If 500 gallons of water are used each day, write the function $f(x)$ that represents the amount of water in the tank *x* days after it is full.

   _____

LESSON 6-4

Slope-Intercept Form

Reteach

An equation is in **slope-intercept form** if it is written as:

$$y = mx + b.$$

m is the slope.
b is the *y*-intercept.

You can use the slope and *y*-intercept to graph a line.

Write $2x + 6y = 12$ in slope-intercept form. Then graph the line.

Step 1: Solve for *y*.

$2x + 6y = 12$ *Subtract 2x from both sides.*

$\underline{-2x \qquad -2x}$

$6y = -2x + 12$

$\dfrac{6y}{6} = \dfrac{-2x + 12}{6}$ *Divide both sides by 6.*

$y = -\dfrac{1}{3}x + 2$ *Simplify.*

Step 2: Find the slope and *y*-intercept.

slope: $m = -\dfrac{1}{3} = \dfrac{-1}{3}$

y-intercept: $b = 2$

Step 3: Graph the line.

• Plot (0, 2).

• Then count 1 **down** (because the rise is **negative**) and 3 **right** (because the run is **positive**) and plot another point.

• Draw a line connecting the points.

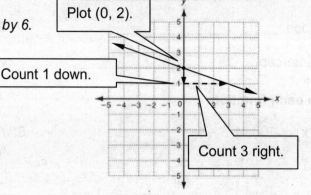

Plot (0, 2).

Count 1 down.

Count 3 right.

Find each slope and *y*-intercept. Then graph each equation.

1. $y = \dfrac{1}{2}x - 3$

2. $3x + y = 2$

3. $2x - y = 3$

_____   _____   _____

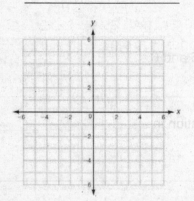   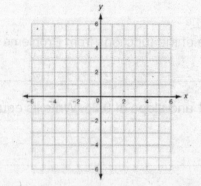   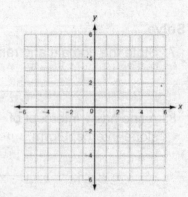

Name _____ Date _____ Class _____

Comparing Linear Functions
Practice and Problem Solving: A/B

The linear functions $f(x)$ and $g(x)$ are defined by the graph and the table below. Assume that the domain of $g(x)$ includes all real numbers between the least and greatest values of x shown in the table.

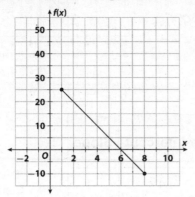

x	g(x)
1	35
2	30
3	25
4	20
5	15
6	10
7	5
8	0

1. Find the domain of $f(x)$.

_____

2. Find the domain of $g(x)$.

_____

3. Find the range of $f(x)$.

_____

4. Find the range of $g(x)$.

_____

5. Find the initial value of $f(x)$.

_____

6. Find the initial value of $g(x)$.

_____

7. Find the slope of the line represented by $f(x)$.

_____

8. Find the slope of the line represented by $g(x)$.

_____

9. How are $f(x)$ and $g(x)$ alike? How are they different?

_____

_____

10. Describe a situation that could be represented by $f(x)$.

_____

11. Describe a situation that could be represented by $g(x)$.

_____

12. If the domains of $f(x)$ and $g(x)$ were extended to include all real numbers greater than or equal to 0, what would their y-intercepts be?

_____

Name _____ Date _____ Class _____

LESSON 6-5

Comparing Linear Functions
Reteach

You can describe a **linear function** with a table, a graph, or an equation.

The table shows $f(x)$.

x	–1	0	1	2	3	4
f(x)	5	4	3	2	1	0

The graph shows $g(x)$.

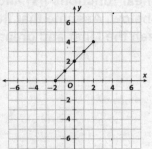

This chart compares $f(x)$ and $g(x)$.

	Domain	Range	Initial (starting) value of $f(x)$	y-intercept	Slope
f(x)	from –1 to 4	from 5 to 0	5	4	–1
g(x)	from –2 to 2	from 0 to 4	0	2	1

Complete each chart. Assume that the domain of $f(x)$ includes all real numbers between the least and greatest values of x.

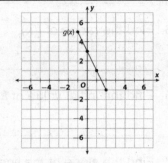

1.

x	–4	–2	0	1
f(x)	4	0	–4	–6

	Domain	Range	Initial (starting) value of $f(x)$	y-intercept	Slope
f(x)					
g(x)					

2.

x	–1	0	1	2	3	4
f(x)	–3	–2	–1	0	1	2

$h(x) = x + 1$, for $-2 \leq x \leq 2$

	Domain	Range	Initial (starting) value of $f(x)$	y-intercept	Slope
f(x)					
h(x)					

LESSON 6-6
Transforming Linear Functions
Practice and Problem Solving: A/B

Identify the steeper line.

1. $y = 3x + 4$ or $y = 6x + 11$

2. $y = -5x - 1$ or $y = -2x - 7$

_____

_____

Each transformation is performed on the line with equation $y = 2x - 1$. Write the equation of the new line.

3. vertical translation down 3 units

4. slope increased by 4

_____

_____

5. slope cut in half

6. shifted up 1 unit

_____

_____

7. slope increased by 50%

8. shifted up 3 units and slope doubled

_____

_____

A salesperson earns a base salary of $4,000 per month plus 15% commission on sales. Her monthly income, $f(s)$, is given by the function $f(s) = 4000 + 0.15s$, where s is monthly sales, in dollars. Use this information for Problems 9–12.

9. Find $g(s)$ if the salesperson's commission is lowered to 5%

_____

10. Find $h(s)$ if the salesperson's base salary is doubled.

_____

11. Find $k(s)$ if the salesperson's base salary is cut in half and her commission is doubled.

_____

12. Graph $f(s)$ and $k(s)$ on the coordinate grid below.

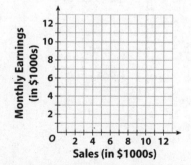

LESSON 6-6

Transforming Linear Functions

Reteach

For a linear function $f(x) = mx + b$, changing the value of b moves the graph up or down.

Description	Equation	y-intercept or b
Parent function	$f(x) = x$	0
Translate up 2	$g(x) = x + 2$	2
Translate down 4	$h(x) = x - 4$	−4

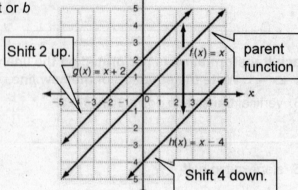

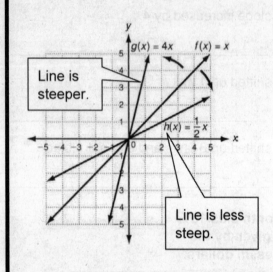

Changing the absolute value of the slope m makes the line more or less steep.

If m is **positive**, the line goes **up** from left to right.

If m is **negative**, the line goes **down** from left to right.

Predict the change in the graph from $f(x)$ to $g(x)$.
Then graph both lines to check your prediction.

1. $f(x) = x$; $g(x) = x + 5$

_____

2. $f(x) = -3x + 1$; $g(x) = 3x + 1$

_____

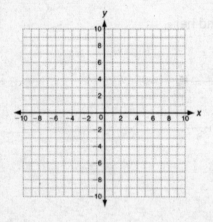

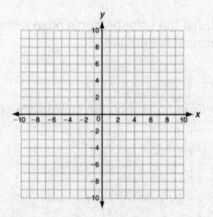

**LESSON
6-7**
Writing Linear Functions
Practice and Problem Solving: A/B

Write each linear function using the given information.

1. The graph of the function has slope of $\frac{1}{2}$ and *y*-intercept of –6.

   _____

2. The graph of the function has slope of –9 and *y*-intercept of –3.

   _____

3.

x	f(x)
–2	18
1	9
4	0

4.

x	f(x)
–5	–9
–2	–7
4	–3

   _____

   _____

5.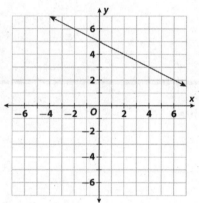

6.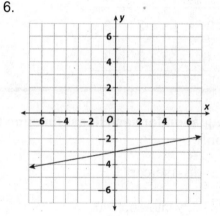

   _____

   _____

Solve.

7. The amount that a consultant charges for her work can be modeled using a linear function. For 4 hours of work, the consultant charges $400. For 5 hours of work, she charges $450. Write the function, $f(h)$, that represents the amount the consultant charges for h hours of work.

   _____

8. When it was 70 degrees outside, 50 members showed up at a beach club. For each degree the temperature rose, another 10 members came to the beach club. Write the function, $f(t)$, that represents the number of members at the beach club as a function of the temperature.

   _____

LESSON 6-7
Writing Linear Functions
Reteach

An equation is in **slope-intercept form** if it is written as:

$$y = mx + b.$$

> *m* is the slope.
> *b* is the *y*-intercept.

A line has a slope of −4 and a *y*-intercept of 3. Write the equation in slope-intercept form.

$y = mx + b$ *Substitute the given values for m and b.*

$y = -4x + 3$

Find values for *m* and *b* from a table or graph.

Slope $= m = \dfrac{\text{change in } y\text{-values}}{\text{change in } x\text{-values}}$ between any two points on the line.

At the *y*-intercept, $x = 0$ and $y = b$.

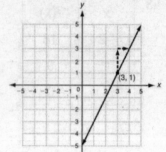

Example: The linear function in this graph is $f(x) = 2x - 5$.

Example: The linear function in this table is $f(x) = 3x - 6$.

x	0	1	2	3
f(x)	−6	−3	0	3

Write an equation for each linear function *f*(x) using the given information.

1. slope $= \dfrac{1}{4}$, *y*-intercept = 3   _____

2. slope = −5, *y*-intercept = 0   _____

3. slope = 7, *y*-intercept = −2   _____

4.   _____

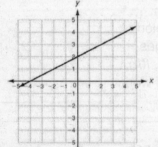

5.   _____

x	−1	0	1	2
f(x)	−4	−2	0	2

LESSON 7-1 Arithmetic Sequences

Practice and Problem Solving: A/B

Write an explicit rule and a recursive rule for each sequence.

1.

n	1	2	3	4	5
$f(n)$	8	12	16	20	24

_____

_____

2.

n	1	2	3	4	5
$f(n)$	11	7	3	−1	−5

_____

_____

3.

n	1	2	3	4	5
$f(n)$	−20	−13	−6	1	8

_____

_____

4.

n	1	2	3	4	5
$f(n)$	2.7	4.3	5.9	7.5	9.1

_____

_____

5.

n	1	2	3	4	5
$f(n)$	1	−8	−17	−26	−35

_____

_____

6.

n	1	2	3	4	5
$f(n)$	−3	2.5	8	13.5	19

_____

_____

Solve.

7. The explicit rule for an arithmetic sequence is $f(n) = 13 + 6(n − 1)$.
   Find the first four terms of the sequence.

_____

8. Helene paid back $100 in Month 1 of her loan. In each month after
   that, Helene paid back $50. Write an explicit formula and a recursive
   formula that shows $f(n)$, the total amount Helene had paid back by
   Month n.

_____

9. The explicit rule for an arithmetic sequence is $f(n) = 18 + 5(n − 1)$.
   Write a recursive rule for this sequence.

_____

10. A recursive rule for an arithmetic sequence is $f(1) = 7$, $f(n) =$
    $f(n − 1) + 47$ for $n \geq 2$. Write an explicit rule for this sequence.

_____

LESSON 7-1 Arithmetic Sequences
Reteach

An **arithmetic sequence** is a list of numbers (or **terms**) with a **common difference** between each number.

0, 6, 12, 18, ...

+6 +6 +6 — Find how much you add or subtract to move from term to term.

The difference between terms is constant.

In this example, $f(1) = 0$, $f(2) = 6$, $f(3) = 12$, $f(4) = 18$, ...
The common difference is 6.

Use the common difference, d, to write rules for an arithmetic sequence.

A **recursive** rule has this general form: Given $f(1)$, $f(n) = f(n - 1) + d$ for $n \geq 2$

Substitute $d = 6$: $f(n) = f(n - 1) + 6$ for $n \geq 2$

An **explicit** rule has this general form: $f(n) = f(1) + d(n - 1)$

Substitute $d = 6$ from the example: $f(n) = f(1) + 6(n - 1)$

Indicate whether each sequence is arithmetic. If so, find the common difference, and write an explicit rule for the sequence.

1. −1, 2, −3, 4, ...   2. 14, 12, 10, 8, ...   3. 3, 6, 9, 27, ...

_____   _____   _____

_____   _____   _____

Write a recursive rule and an explicit rule for each sequence.

4. −5, 0, 5, 10, ...   5. 7, 4, 1, −2, ...   6. 4, 7, 10, 13, ...

_____   _____   _____

_____   _____   _____

Use the explicit rule given to write the first three terms for each sequence.

7. $f(n) = 6 + 3(n - 1)$ 8. $f(n) = 16 + \left(-\frac{1}{2}\right)(n - 1)$ 9. $f(n) = 20 + (-10)(n - 1)$

_____   _____   _____

LESSON 7-2

Operations with Linear Functions

Practice and Problem Solving: A/B

Given the functions $f(x)$ and $g(x)$, find the function $h(x) = f(x) + g(x)$.

1. $f(x) = 3x - 2$, $g(x) = 12x + 5$

2. $f(x) = -6x - 1$, $g(x) = 3x - 4$

_____

_____

Given the functions $f(x)$ and $g(x)$, find the function $k(x) = f(x) - g(x)$.

3. $f(x) = 8x + 7$, $g(x) = 5x + 3$

4. $f(x) = 2x + 6$, $g(x) = -4x + 11$

_____

_____

Given the functions $f(x)$ and $g(x)$, find the function $p(x) = f(x) \times g(x)$.

5. $f(x) = -5$, $g(x) = -9x - 4$

6. $f(x) = \dfrac{1}{3}$, $g(x) = 12x - 27$

_____

_____

A company manufactures and sells slippers. The price it charges wholesalers is $18 per pair. The company has fixed annual costs of $30,000. In addition, it costs the company $4.50 to make each pair of slippers. Use this information for Problems 7–12.

7. Write the revenue function $r(x)$, where x is the number of slippers sold in a year and $r(x)$ is the total revenue from those sales.

_____

8. Write the cost function $c(x)$, where x is the number of slippers sold in a year and $c(x)$ is the annual cost for the company.

_____

9. Profit equals the difference between revenue and cost. Write the profit

function, $p(x)$, for this company. _____

10. In 2010, the company sold 2000 pairs of slippers. Find its profit or loss.

_____

11. In 2012, the company sold 15,000 pairs of slippers. Find its profit or loss.

_____

12. Suppose material costs rise and it now costs $5.25 to make a pair of slippers. The company decides to raise its price from $18 to $19. Write its new profit function.

_____

LESSON 7-2 Operations with Linear Functions
Reteach

Adding or subtracting functions and multiplying by a constant function are the same as operations with algebraic expressions.

Find the sum $h(x) = f(x) + g(x)$ when $f(x) = 2x + 3$ and $g(x) = -x - 2$.

$$h(x) = f(x) + g(x)$$

Substitute:	$h(x) = (2x + 3) + (-x - 2)$
Remove parentheses:	$h(x) = 2x + 3 - x - 2$
Collect terms:	$h(x) = 2x - x + 3 - 2$
Simplify:	$h(x) = x + 1$

Find the difference $h(x) = f(x) - g(x)$ when $f(x) = 2x + 3$ and $g(x) = -x - 2$.

$$h(x) = f(x) - g(x)$$

Substitute:	$h(x) = (2x + 3) - (-x - 2)$
Remove parentheses:	$h(x) = 2x + 3 + x + 2$
Collect terms:	$h(x) = 2x + x + 3 + 2$
Simplify:	$h(x) = 3x + 5$

Find the product $h(x) = f(x) \times g(x)$ when $f(x) = -4$ and $g(x) = -3x + 1$.

$$h(x) = f(x) \times g(x)$$

Substitute:	$h(x) = (-4) \times (-3x + 1)$
Multiply:	$h(x) = (-4)(-3x) + (-4)(1)$
Simplify:	$h(x) = 12x - 4$

Given the functions $f(x) = 7x + 4$ and $g(x) = 3x + 2$, find $h(x) = f(x) + g(x)$ and $j(x) = f(x) - g(x)$.

1.

$h(x) =$ _____

2.

$j(x) =$ _____

Given the functions $f(x) = 3x - 6$ and $g(x) = x - 4$, find $h(x) = f(x) + g(x)$ and $j(x) = f(x) - g(x)$.

3.

$h(x) =$ _____

4.

$j(x) =$ _____

Given the functions $f(x) = 3$ and $g(x) = 5x + 4$, find $k(x) = f(x) \times g(x)$.

5.

$k(x) =$ _____

Given the functions $f(x) = -6$ and $g(x) = 3x - 2$, find $k(x) = f(x) \times g(x)$.

6.

$k(x) =$ _____

LESSON
7-3

Linear Functions and Their Inverses
Practice and Problem Solving: A/B

Each graph shows a linear function. Find an equation for its inverse and graph its inverse.

1.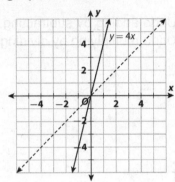

   $y = 4x$

   _____

2.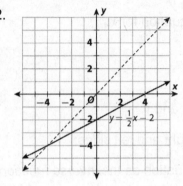

   $y = \frac{1}{2}x - 2$

   _____

3.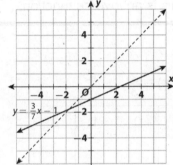

   $y = \frac{3}{7}x - 1$

   _____

4.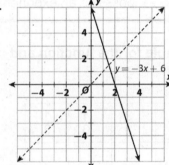

   $y = -3x + 6$

   _____

An online ticket seller charges $44 for each ticket to a concert, plus a handling fee of $12 per order, no matter how many tickets are purchased. Use this information for Problems 5–8.

5. Write $f(x)$, the function you can use to find the cost of x tickets.

   _____

6. Find $f^{-1}(x)$.

   _____

7. Explain what the function $f^{-1}(x)$ represents.

   _____

8. Find $f^{-1}(320)$ and explain what it represents.

   _____

Linear Functions and Their Inverses
Reteach

Inverse operations *undo* each other. The inverse of adding 7 is subtracting 7.

To find the **inverse of a function**, such as $\qquad f(x) = 3x + 2,$

Rewrite with *y*: $\qquad\qquad\qquad\qquad\qquad y = 3x + 2$

Solve the equation for *x*: $\qquad\qquad\qquad \dfrac{-2 = \quad -2}{}$ Undo adding by subtracting.

$$\dfrac{y - 2 =}{3} \quad \dfrac{3x}{3} \qquad \text{Undo multiplying by dividing.}$$

Simplify: $\qquad\qquad\qquad\qquad\qquad \frac{1}{3}(y) - \frac{2}{3} = x$

Switch the *x* and *y*: $\qquad\qquad\qquad \frac{1}{3}(x) - \frac{2}{3} = y$

Exchange right and left sides: $\qquad\qquad y = \frac{1}{3}(x) - \frac{2}{3}$

Write the equation as the *inverse function*: $\quad f^{-1}(x) = \frac{1}{3}(x) - \frac{2}{3}$

Say $f^{-1}(x) = \frac{1}{3}(x) - \frac{2}{3}$ like this: "The inverse function of *x* is one third *x* minus two thirds."

Even though the −1 looks like an exponent, it is *not*. It tells you this is an *inverse* function.

Complete the table for the function and its inverse.

1. $f(x) = 3x + 2$

x	−1	$-\frac{2}{3}$	$-\frac{1}{3}$	$\frac{1}{3}$
f(x)				

2. $f^{-1}(x) = \frac{1}{3}(x) - \frac{2}{3}$

x	−1	0	1	3
f(x)				

Compare the domain and range for the two tables above.

3.

_____

Find the inverse function for each linear function.

4. $f(x) = 2x - 8$ 5. $f(x) = -3x + 4$ 6. $f(x) = x$

_____   _____   _____

LESSON 7-4 Linear Inequalities in Two Variables

Practice and Problem Solving: A/B

Use substitution to tell whether each ordered pair is a solution of the given inequality.

1. $(3, 4)$; $y > x + 2$ 2. $(4, 2)$; $y \le 2x - 3$ 3. $(2, -1)$; $y < -x$

_____   _____   _____

Rewrite each linear inequality in slope-intercept form. Then graph the solutions in the coordinate plane.

4. $y - x \le 3$

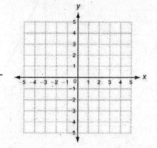

_____

5. $6x + 2y > -2$

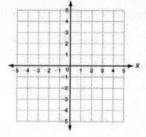

_____

6. Trey is buying peach and blueberry yogurt cups. He will buy at most 8 cups of yogurt. Let x be the number of peach yogurt cups and y be the number of blueberry yogurt cups he buys.

   a. Write an inequality to describe the situation.

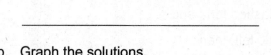

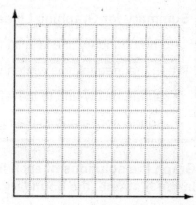

   b. Graph the solutions.

   c. Give two possible combinations of peach and blueberry yogurt that Trey can choose.

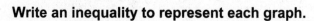

_____

Write an inequality to represent each graph.

7.

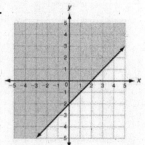

_____

8.

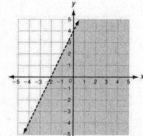

_____

9.

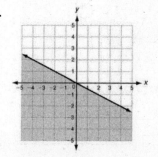

_____

Linear Inequalities in Two Variables

Reteach

To graph a linear inequality:

Step 1: Solve the inequality for *y*.

Step 2: Graph the boundary line. If ≤ or ≥ use a solid line. If < or > use a dashed line.

Step 3: Determine which side to shade.

Graph the solutions of 2*x* + *y* ≤ 4.

Step 1: Solve for y. $2x + y \le 4$

$$\underline{-2x \quad -2x}$$

$$y \le -2x + 4$$

Step 2: Graph the boundary line.

Use a solid line for ≤.

Step 3: Determine which side to shade.

Substitute (0, 0) into $2x + y \le 4$.

$$2x + y \le 4$$

$$2(0) + 0 \overset{?}{\le} 4$$

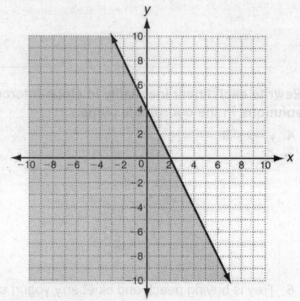

$0 \overset{?}{\le} 4$. The statement is true. Shade the side that contains the point (0, 0).

Summary for Graphing Linear Inequalities in Two Variables

• The boundary line is solid for ≤ and ≥ and dashed for < and >.

When the inequality is written with *y* alone on the left, then

• shade below and to the left of the line for < and ≤,

• shade above and to the right of the line for > and ≥.

Graph the solutions of each linear inequality.
In the first one, the boundary line is already drawn.

1. $y < -2x - 9$

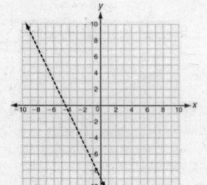

2. $y - x < 3$

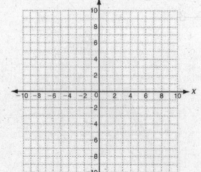

3. $x + y + 2 \ge 0$

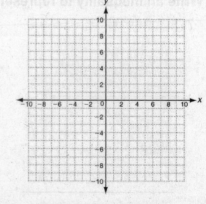

LESSON
8-1

Correlation

Practice and Problem Solving: A/B

1. The table shows the number of soft drinks sold at a small restaurant from 11:00 am to 1:00 pm. Graph a scatter plot using the given data.

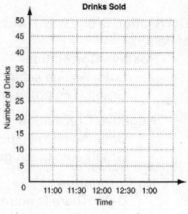

Time of Day	11:00	11:30	12:00	12:30	1:00
Number of Drinks	20	29	34	49	44

Write *positive*, *negative*, or *none* to describe the correlation illustrated by each scatter plot.

2.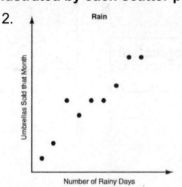

_____

3.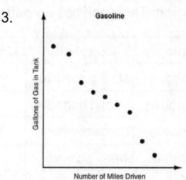

_____

Identify the correlation you would expect to see between each pair of data sets. Explain.

4. the temperature during the day and the number of people in the pool

_____

_____

5. the height of an algebra student and the number of phone calls they make in one week

_____

_____

Solve.

6. During one season, a researcher collected data on the number of hot chocolate vendors at football stadiums and the outside temperature. Noticing a strong negative correlation, he concluded that hot chocolate vendors cause temperatures to fall. What would you have concluded?

_____

_____

LESSON 8-1 Correlation
Reteach

Correlation is one way to describe the relationship between two sets of data.

Positive Correlation
Data: As one set **increases**, the other set **increases**.
Graph: The graph **goes up** from left to right.

Negative Correlation
Data: As one set **increases**, the other set **decreases**.
Graph: The graph **goes down** from left to right.

No Correlation
Data: There is **no relationship** between the sets.
Graph: The graph has **no pattern**.

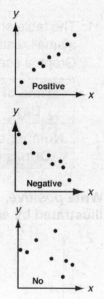

Example	Correlation	Correlation Coefficient (*estimated*)
1st graph *above*	strong positive	+1
2nd graph *above*	strong negative	−1
3rd graph *above*	no correlation	0
4th graph *below*	weak positive	+0.5
5th graph *below*	weak negative	−0.5

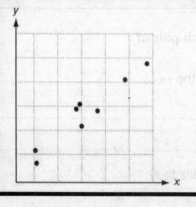 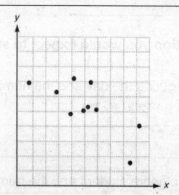

Estimate the correlation coefficient for each scatter plot as −1, −0.5, 0, 0.5, or 1.

1.

2.

3.

_____   _____   _____

LESSON
8-2
Fitting Lines to Data
Practice and Problem Solving: A/B

The table below lists the ages and heights of ten children. Use the data for Problems 1–5.

A, age in years	2	3	3	4	4	4	5	5	5	6
H, height in inches	30	33	34	37	35	38	40	42	43	42

1. Draw a scatter plot and line of fit for the data.

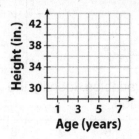

2. A student fit the line $H = 3.5A + 23$ to the data. Graph the student's line above. Then calculate the student's predicted values and residuals.

A, age in years	2	3	3	4	4	4	5	5	5	6
H, height in inches	30	33	34	37	35	38	40	42	43	42
Predicted Values										
Residuals										

3. Use the graph below to make a residual plot.

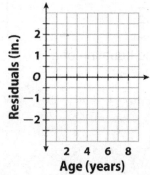

4. Use your residual plot to discuss how well the student's line fits the data.

_____

_____

5. Use the student's line to predict the height of a man 20 years old. Discuss the reasonableness of the result.

_____

_____

_____

Fitting Lines to Data
Reteach

Use a scatter plot to identify a correlation. If the variables appear
correlated, then find a line of fit.

Positive correlation	Negative correlation	No correlation
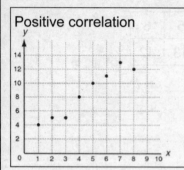	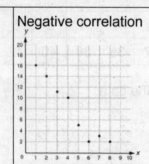	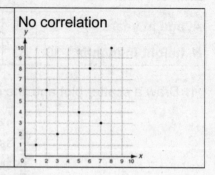

The table shows the relationship between two variables. Identify the
correlation, sketch a line of fit, and find its equation.

x	1	2	3	4	5	6	7	8
y	16	14	11	10	5	2	3	2

Step 1   Make a scatter plot of the data.
As *x* increases, *y* decreases.
The data is negatively correlated.

Step 2   Use a straightedge to draw a line.
There will be some points above and below the line.

Step 3   Choose two points on the line to find the equation:
(1, 16) and (7, 2).

Step 4   Use the points to find the slope:

$$m = \frac{\text{change in } y}{\text{change in } x} = \frac{16-2}{1-7} = \frac{14}{-6} = -\frac{7}{3}$$

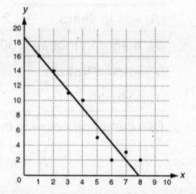

Step 5   Use the point-slope form to find the equation of a
line that models the data.

$$y - y_1 = m(x - x_1)$$
$$y - 2 = -\frac{7}{3}(x - 7)$$
$$y = -\frac{7}{3}x + \frac{55}{3}$$

Use the scatter plot of the data to solve.

1. The correlation is _____.

2. Choose two points on the line and find the slope.

_____

3. Find the equation of a line that models the data.

_____

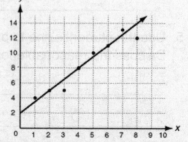

Name _____ Date _____ Class_____

Linear Regression

Practice and Problem Solving: A/B

Use the points below for Problems 1–6.

x	2	3	5	5	6	7	8	8
y	2	1	2	3	5	4	3	5

1. Plot the points as ordered pairs on the coordinate grid below. Then graph and label these two lines of fit for the data:
$y = 0.5x + 0.5$ and $y = x - 2$.

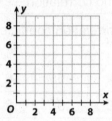

2. Complete the table for $y = 0.5x + .0.5$.

x	y (actual)	y (predicted)	residual	square of residual

3. Complete the table for $y = x - 2$.

x	y (actual)	y (predicted)	residual	square of residual

4. Which line fits the data better? Explain.

_____

_____

5. Go back to the original data. Use a calculator to find the equation of the least squares line of best fit. Round the slope and *y*-intercept to two decimal places.

_____

_____

6. Does your answer from Problem 5 validate or invalidate your answer from Problem 4? Explain.

_____

_____

LESSON 8-3 Linear Regression
Reteach

A line of best fit can be used to predict data.
Use the correlation coefficient, *r*, to measure how well the data fits.

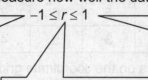

$-1 \leq r \leq 1$

| If *r* is near –1, data is modeled by a line with a negative slope. | | If *r* is near 1, data is modeled by a line with a positive slope. |

If *r* is near 0, data has no correlation.

Use a graphing calculator to find the correlation coefficient of the data and the line of best fit.
Use STAT EDIT to enter the data.

x	1	2	3	4	5	6	7	8
y	16	14	11	10	5	2	3	2

Use LinReg from the STAT CALC menu to find the line of best fit and the correlation coefficient.

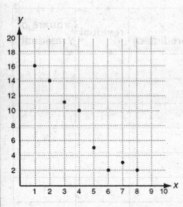

LinReg

$y = ax + b$

$a = -2.202$

$b = 17.786$

$r^2 = .9308$

$r = -.9648$

The correlation coefficient is –0.9648. The data is very close to linear with a negative slope.

Use the linear regression model to predict *y* when *x* = 3.5.

$y \approx -2.2x + 17.79$

$y \approx -2.2 \,(3.5) + 17.79$

$y \approx 10.09$

Use a calculator and the scatter plot of the data to solve.

1. Find the correlation coefficient, *r*. _____

2. Find the equation of the line of best fit.

   _____

3. Predict *y* when *x* = 2.6. _____

4. Predict *y* when *x* = 5.3. _____

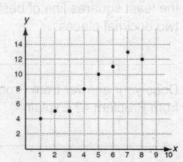

Name _____ Date _____ Class_____

Solving Linear Systems by Graphing

Practice and Problem Solving: A/B

Tell whether the ordered pair is a solution of the given system.

1. $(3, 1)$; $\begin{cases} x + 3y = 6 \\ 4x - 5y = 7 \end{cases}$ _____

2. $(6, -2)$; $\begin{cases} 3x - 2y = 14 \\ 5x - y = 32 \end{cases}$ _____

$x + 3y = 6$	$4x - 5y = 7$	$3x - 2y = 14$	$5x - y = 32$

Solve each system by graphing. Check your answer.

3. $\begin{cases} y = x + 4 \\ y = -2x + 1 \end{cases}$ Solution:_____

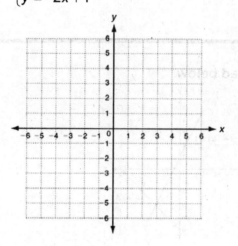

4. $\begin{cases} y = x + 6 \\ y = -3x + 6 \end{cases}$ Solution:_____

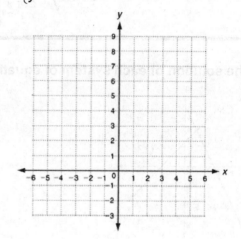

5. Maryann and Carlos are each saving for new scooters. So far, Maryann has $9 saved, and can earn $6 per hour babysitting. Carlos has $3 saved, and can earn $9 per hour working at his family's restaurant. After how many hours of work will Maryann and Carlos have saved the same amount? What will that amount be?

_____

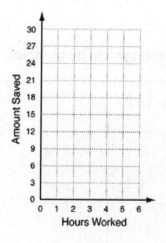

LESSON 9-1 Solving Linear Systems by Graphing
Reteach

Graph to check if (5, 7) is a solution of $\begin{cases} y = x + 2 \\ y = 2x + 3 \end{cases}$.

If (5, 7) is not the solution, find the solution from the graph.

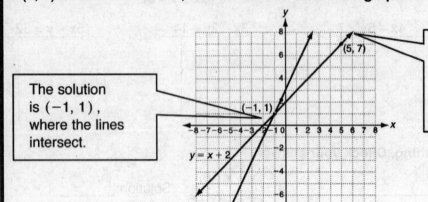

The solution is (−1, 1), where the lines intersect.

(5, 7) satisfies one equation but not the other. Therefore, (5, 7) is not a solution of this system.

Find the solution of each system of equations graphed below.

1.

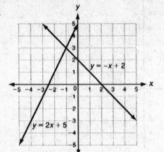

_____

2.

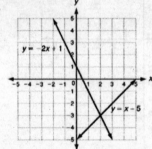

_____

Solve each system by graphing.

3. $\begin{cases} y = -3 \\ y = x + 2 \end{cases}$

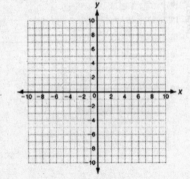

_____

4. $\begin{cases} y = x - 6 \\ y = -x \end{cases}$

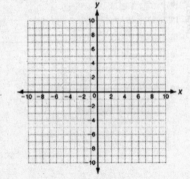

_____

LESSON 9-2

Solving Linear Systems by Substitution
Practice and Problem Solving: A/B

Solve each system by substitution. Check your answer.

1. $\begin{cases} y = x - 2 \\ y = 4x + 1 \end{cases}$

2. $\begin{cases} y = x - 4 \\ y = -x + 2 \end{cases}$

3. $\begin{cases} y = 3x + 1 \\ y = 5x - 3 \end{cases}$

_____

4. $\begin{cases} 2x - y = 6 \\ x + y = -3 \end{cases}$

5. $\begin{cases} 2x + y = 8 \\ y = x - 7 \end{cases}$

6. $\begin{cases} 2x + 3y = 0 \\ x + 2y = -1 \end{cases}$

_____

7. $\begin{cases} 3x - 2y = 7 \\ x + 3y = -5 \end{cases}$

8. $\begin{cases} -2x + y = 0 \\ 5x + 3y = -11 \end{cases}$

9. $\begin{cases} \dfrac{1}{2}x + \dfrac{1}{3}y = 5 \\ \dfrac{1}{4}x + y = 10 \end{cases}$

_____

Write a system of equations to solve.

10. A woman's age is three years more than twice her son's age. The sum of their ages is 84. How old is the son?

_____

11. The length of a rectangle is three times its width. The perimeter of the rectangle is 100 inches. What are the dimensions of the rectangle?

_____

12. Efrem worked 40 hours at his two jobs last week. He earned $20 per hour at his weekday job and $18 per hour at his weekend. He earned $770 in all. How many hours did he work at each job?

_____

LESSON 9-2
Solving Linear Systems by Substitution
Reteach

You can use substitution to solve a system of equations if one of the equations is already solved for a variable.

Solve $\begin{cases} y = x + 2 \\ 3x + y = 10 \end{cases}$

Step 1: Choose the equation to use as the substitute.

Use the first equation $y = x + 2$ because it is already solved for a variable.

Step 2: Solve by substitution.

$$\boxed{x + 2}$$

$$3x + y = 10$$
$$3x + (x + 2) = 10 \qquad \textit{Substitute } x + 2 \textit{ for } y.$$
$$4x + 2 = 10 \qquad \textit{Combine like terms.}$$
$$\frac{-2}{4x} = \frac{-2}{8}$$
$$\frac{4x}{4} = \frac{8}{4}$$
$$x = 2$$

Step 3: Now substitute $x = 2$ back into one of the original equations to find the value of y.

$$y = x + 2$$
$$y = 2 + 2$$
$$y = 4$$

The solution is (2, 4).

Check:
Substitute (2, 4) into both equations.

$$y = x + 2 \qquad\qquad 3x + y = 10$$
$$4 \overset{?}{=} 2 + 2 \qquad\qquad 3(2) + 4 \overset{?}{=} 10$$
$$4 \overset{?}{=} 4 \checkmark \qquad\qquad 6 + 4 \overset{?}{=} 10$$
$$\qquad\qquad\qquad 10 \overset{?}{=} 10 \checkmark$$

You may need to solve one of the equations for a variable before solving with substitution.

Solve each system by substitution.

1. $\begin{cases} y = x + 2 \\ y = 2x - 5 \end{cases}$

2. $\begin{cases} x = y + 10 \\ x = 2y + 3 \end{cases}$

3. $\begin{cases} x - y = -3 \\ 2x + y = 12 \end{cases}$

4. $\begin{cases} y - x = 8 \\ 5x + 2y = 9 \end{cases}$

Name _____ Date _____ Class _____

Solving Linear Systems by Adding or Subtracting
Practice and Problem Solving: A/B

Solve each system of linear equations by adding or subtracting. Check your answer.

1. $x - 5y = 10$
   $2x + 5y = 5$

2. $x + y = -10$
   $5x + y = -2$

3. $4x + 10y = 2$
   $-4x + 8y = 16$

4. $-3x - 7y = 8$
   $3x - 2y = -44$

5. $-x + 4y = 15$
   $3x + 4y = 3$

6. $-4x + 11y = 5$
   $4x - 11y = -5$

7. $-x - y = 1$
   $-x + y = -1$

8. $3x - 5y = 60$
   $4x + 5y = -4$

Write a system of equations to solve.

9. A plumber charges an initial amount to make a house call plus an hourly rate for the time he is working. A 1-hour job costs $90 and a 3-hour job costs $210. What is the initial amount and the hourly rate that the plumber charges?

10. A man and his three children spent $40 to attend a show. A second family of three children and their two parents spent $53 for the same show. How much does a child's ticket cost?

Name _____ Date _____ Class_____

LESSON 9-3

Solving Linear Systems by Adding or Subtracting
Reteach

To use the **elimination method** to solve a system of linear equations:
1. Add or subtract the equations to eliminate one variable.
2. Solve the resulting equation for the other variable.
3. Substitute the value for the known variable into one of the original equations.
4. Solve for the other variable.
5. Check the values in both equations.

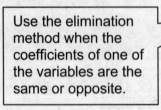

Use the elimination method when the coefficients of one of the variables are the same or opposite.

$$\begin{cases} 3x + 2y = 7 \\ 5x - 2y = 1 \end{cases}$$

The y-terms have opposite coefficients, so add.

$$\begin{aligned} 3x + 2y &= 7 \\ +5x - 2y &= 1 \\ \hline 8x &= 8 \\ x &= 1 \end{aligned}$$

Add the equations.

Solve for x.

Substitute $x = 1$ into $3x + 2y = 7$ and solve for y:

$$\begin{aligned} 3x + 2y &= 7 \\ 3(1) + 2y &= 7 \\ 2y &= 4 \\ y &= 2 \end{aligned}$$

The solution to the system is the ordered pair (1, 2).

Check using both equations:

$$3x + 2y = 7 \qquad\qquad 5x - 2y = 1$$

$$3(1) + 2(2) \overset{?}{=} 7 \qquad 5(1) - 2(2) \overset{?}{=} 1$$

$$7 = 7\checkmark \qquad\qquad 1 = 1\checkmark$$

Solve each system by adding or subtracting.

1. $\begin{cases} -2x - y = -5 \\ 3x + y = -1 \end{cases}$

2. $\begin{cases} 3x + 2y = 10 \\ 3x - 2y = 14 \end{cases}$

_____

3. $\begin{cases} x + y = 12 \\ 2x + y = 6 \end{cases}$

4. $\begin{cases} 2x + y = 1 \\ -2x - 3y = 5 \end{cases}$

_____

Name _____ Date _____ Class_____

LESSON 9-4

Solving Linear Systems by Multiplying
Practice and Problem Solving: A/B

Solve each system of equations. Check your answer.

1. $\begin{cases} -3x - 4y = -2 \\ 6x + 4y = 3 \end{cases}$

2. $\begin{cases} 2x - 2y = 14 \\ x + 4y = -13 \end{cases}$

_____

3. $\begin{cases} y - x = 17 \\ 2y + 3x = -11 \end{cases}$

4. $\begin{cases} x + 6y = 1 \\ 2x - 3y = 32 \end{cases}$

_____

5. $\begin{cases} 3x + y = -15 \\ 2x - 3y = 23 \end{cases}$

6. $\begin{cases} 5x - 2y = -48 \\ 2x + 3y = -23 \end{cases}$

_____

7. $\begin{cases} 4x - 3y = -9 \\ 5x - y = 8 \end{cases}$

8. $\begin{cases} 3x - 3y = -1 \\ 12x - 2y = 16 \end{cases}$

_____

Solve.

9. Ten bagels and four muffins cost $13. Five bagels and eight muffins cost $14. How much does a bagel cost? How much does a muffin cost?

_____

10. John can service a television and a cable box in one hour. It took him four hours yesterday to service two televisions and ten cable boxes. How many minutes does John need to service a cable box?

_____

LESSON 9-4 Solving Linear Systems by Multiplying
Reteach

To solve a system by elimination, you may first need to multiply *one* of the equations to make the coefficients match.

$$\begin{cases} 2x + 5y = 9 \\ x - 3y = 10 \end{cases}$$

Multiply bottom equation by –2.

$$2x + 5y = 9$$
$$-2(x - 3y) = -2(10)$$

$$2x + 5y = 9$$
$$\underline{-2x + 6y = -20}$$
$$0 + 11y = -11$$

Solve for y: $\dfrac{11y}{11} = \dfrac{-11}{11}$
$$y = -1$$

Substitute –1 for y in $x - 3y = 10$.
$$x - 3(-1) = 10$$
$$x + 3 = 10$$
$$\underline{-3 = -3}$$
$$x = 7$$

The solution to the system is the ordered pair (7, –1).

You may need to multiply *both* of the equations to make the coefficients match.

$$\begin{cases} 5x + 3y = 2 \\ 4x + 2y = 10 \end{cases}$$

Multiply the top by –2 and the bottom by 3.

$$-2(5x + 3y = 2)$$
$$3(4x + 2y = 10)$$

$$-10x + (-6y) = -4$$
$$\underline{12x + 6y = 30}$$
$$2x + 0 = 26$$
$$x = 13$$

The solution to this system is the ordered pair (13, –21).

After you multiply, *add or subtract* the two equations.
Solve for the variable that is left.
Substitute to find the value of the other variable.
Check in both equations.

Solve each system by multiplying. Check your answer.

1. $\begin{cases} 2x - 3y = 5 \\ x + 2y = -1 \end{cases}$

2. $\begin{cases} 3x - y = 2 \\ -8x + 2y = 4 \end{cases}$

3. $\begin{cases} 2x + 5y = 22 \\ 10x + 3y = 22 \end{cases}$

4. $\begin{cases} 4x + 2y = 14 \\ 7x - 3y = -8 \end{cases}$

LESSON 9-5

Solving Systems of Linear Inequalities
Practice and Problem Solving: A/B

Tell whether the ordered pair is a solution of the given system.

1. $(2, -2); \begin{cases} y < x - 3 \\ y > -x + 1 \end{cases}$

2. $(2, 5); \begin{cases} y > 2x \\ y \geq x + 2 \end{cases}$

3. $(1, 3); \begin{cases} y \leq x + 2 \\ y > 4x - 1 \end{cases}$

_____   _____   _____

Graph the system of linear inequalities. a. Give two ordered pairs that are solutions. b. Give two ordered pairs that are not solutions.

4. $\begin{cases} y \leq x + 4 \\ y \geq -2x \end{cases}$

5. $\begin{cases} y \leq \dfrac{1}{2}x + 1 \\ x + y < 3 \end{cases}$

6. $\begin{cases} y > x - 4 \\ y < x + 2 \end{cases}$

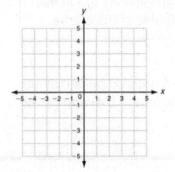   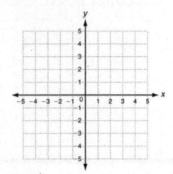   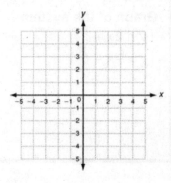

a. _____   a. _____   a. _____

b. _____   b. _____   b. _____

7. Charlene makes $10 per hour babysitting and $5 per hour gardening. She wants to make at least $80 a week, but can work no more than 12 hours a week.

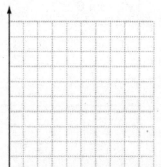

   a. Write a system of linear equations.

   _____

   b. Graph the solutions of the system.

   c. Describe all the possible combinations of hours that Charlene could work at each job.

   _____

   _____

   d. List two possible combinations. _____

   _____

LESSON
9-5

Solving Systems of Linear Inequalities
Reteach

You can graph a system of linear inequalities by combining the graphs of the inequalities.

Graph of $y \leq 2x + 3$ **Graph of** $y > -x - 6$

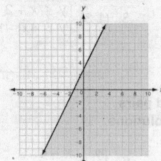   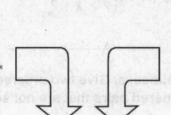   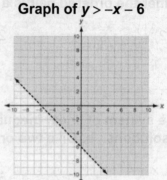

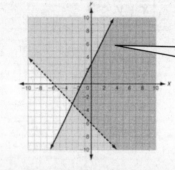

Graph of the system

$$\begin{cases} y \leq 2x + 3 \\ y > -x - 6 \end{cases}$$

All solutions are in this
double shaded area.

Two ordered pairs that are
solutions: (3, 4) and (5, −2)

Solve each system of linear inequalities by graphing. Check your
answer by testing an ordered pair from each region of your graph.

1. $\begin{cases} y > x - 3 \\ y \geq -x + 6 \end{cases}$ 2. $\begin{cases} y < x \\ y > -2x + 1 \end{cases}$ 3. $\begin{cases} y > 2x - 2 \\ y \leq 2x + 3 \end{cases}$

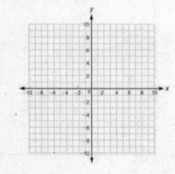   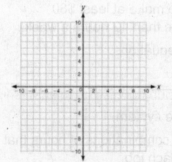   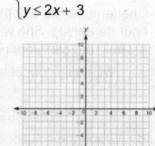

_____   _____   _____

LESSON 10-1

Exponential Functions

Practice and Problem Solving: A/B

Use two points to write an equation for each function shown.

1.

x	0	1	2	3
f(x)	6	18	54	162

2.

x	−2	0	2	4
f(x)	84	21	5.25	1.3125

_____   _____

Graph each function.

3. $y = 5(2)^x$

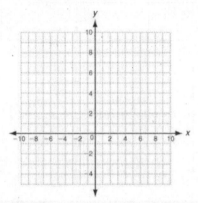

4. $y = -2(3)^x$

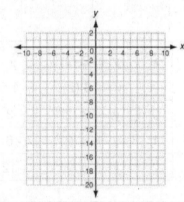

5. $y = 3\left(\dfrac{1}{2}\right)^x$

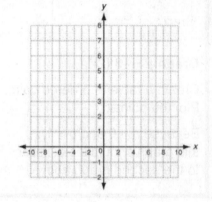

Solve.

6. If a basketball is bounced from a height of 15 feet, the function $f(x) = 15(0.75)^x$ gives the height of the ball in feet of each bounce, where x is the bounce number. What will be the height of the 5th bounce? Round to the nearest tenth of a foot.

_____

7. Starting with 25 members, a club doubled its membership every year. Write the function, $f(n)$, that expresses the number of members in the club after n years. Then find the number of members after six years.

_____

LESSON 10-1

Exponential Functions
Reteach

An exponential function has the form $f(x) = ab^x$.
The independent variable is in an exponent.
The graph is always a curve in two quadrants.

$a \neq 0$
$b > 0$ and $\neq 1$
x is any real number

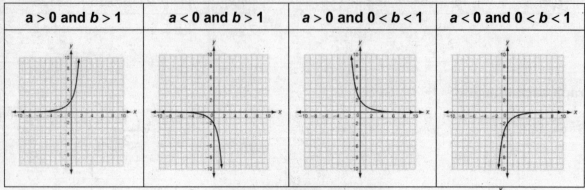

a > 0 and b > 1	a < 0 and b > 1	a > 0 and 0 < b < 1	a < 0 and 0 < b < 1

Graph $y = -3\,(2)^x$.

Create a table of ordered pairs.
Plot the points.

Because $a < 0$ and $b > 1$,
this graph should look similar
to the second graph above.

x	y = -3 (2)ˣ	y
-1	$y = -3\,(2)^{-1}$	-1.5
0	$y = -3\,(2)^0$	-3
1	$y = -3\,(2)^1$	-6
2	$y = -3\,(2)^2$	-12

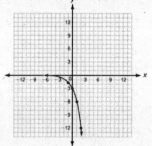

Graph each exponential function.

1. $y = -4\,(0.5)^x$

x	y = -4 (0.5)ˣ	y
-2		
-1		
0		
1		

2. $y = 2\,(5)^x$

x	y = 2 (5)ˣ	y
-1		
0		
1		
2		

3. $y = -1\,(2)^x$

x	y = -1 (2)ˣ	y
-1		
0		
1		
2		

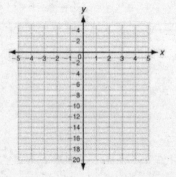
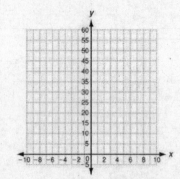
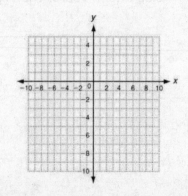

LESSON 10-2

Exponential Growth and Decay

Practice and Problem Solving: A/B

Write an exponential growth function to model each situation. Then find the value of the function after the given amount of time.

1. Annual sales for a fast food restaurant are $650,000 and are increasing at a rate of 4% per year; 5 years

   _____

   _____

2. The population of a school is 800 students and is increasing at a rate of 2% per year; 6 years

   _____

   _____

3. During a certain period of time, about 70 northern sea otters had an annual growth rate of 18%; 4 years

   _____

   _____

Write an exponential decay function to model each situation. Then find the value of the function after the given amount of time.

4. The population of a town is 2500 and is decreasing at a rate of 3% per year; 5 years

   _____

   _____

5. The value of a company's equipment is $25,000 and decreases at a rate of 15% per year; 8 years

   _____

   _____

Write an exponential growth or decay function to model each situation. Then graph each function.

6. The population is 20,000 now and expected to grow at an annual rate of 5%.

   _____

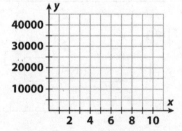

7. A boat that cost $45,000 is depreciating at a rate of 20% per year.

   _____

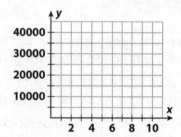

Name _____ Date _____ Class_____

Exponential Growth and Decay
Reteach

In the exponential growth and decay formulas, y = final amount, a = original amount, r = rate of growth or decay, and t = time.

Exponential growth: $y = a(1 + r)^t$ Exponential decay: $y = a(1 - r)^t$

The population of a city is increasing at a rate of 4% each year. In 2000 there were 236,000 people in the city. Write an exponential growth function to model this situation. Then find the population in 2009.	**The population of a city is decreasing at a rate of 6% each year. In 2000 there were 35,000 people in the city. Write an exponential decay function to model this situation. Then find the population in 2012.**
Step 1: Identify the variables.	**Step 1:** Identify the variables.
$a = 236{,}000$ $r = 0.04$	$a = 35{,}000$ $r = 0.06$
Step 2: Substitute for a and r.	**Step 2:** Substitute for a and r.
$y = a(1 + r)^t$	$y = a(1 - r)^t$
$y = 236{,}000(1 + 0.04)^t$	$y = 35{,}000(1 - 0.06)^t$
The exponential growth function is $y = 236{,}000(1.04)^t$.	The exponential decay function is $y = 35{,}000(0.94)^t$.
Growth = greater than 1.	Decay = less than 1.
Step 3: Substitute for t.	**Step 3:** Substitute for t.
$y = 236{,}000(1.04)^9$	$y = 35{,}000(0.94)^{12}$
$\approx 335{,}902$	$\approx 16{,}657$
The population will be about 335,902.	The population will be about 16,657.

Write an exponential growth function to model each situation. Then find the value of the function after the given amount of time.

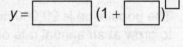

1. Annual sales at a company are $372,000 and increasing at a rate of 5% per year; 8 years

   _____

2. The population of a town is 4200 and increasing at a rate of 3% per year; 7 years

   _____

Write an exponential decay function to model each situation. Then find the value of the function after the given amount of time.

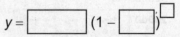

3. Monthly car sales for a certain type of car are $350,000 and are decreasing at a rate of 3% per month; 6 months

   _____

4. An internet chat room has 1200 participants and is decreasing at a rate of 2% per year; 5 years

   _____

LESSON 10-3

Geometric Sequences

Practice and Problem Solving: A/B

Each rule represents a geometric sequence. If the given rule is recursive, write it as an explicit rule. If the rule is explicit, write it as a recursive rule. Assume that $f(1)$ is the first term of the sequence.

1. $f(n) = 11(2)^{n-1}$

2. $f(1) = 2.5; f(n) = f(n-1) \cdot 3.5$ for $n \geq 2$

_____

3. $f(1) = 27; f(n) = f(n-1) \cdot \dfrac{1}{3}$ for $n \geq 2$

4. $f(n) = -4(0.5)^{n-1}$

_____

Write an explicit rule for each geometric sequence based on the given terms from the sequence. Assume that the common ratio r is positive.

5. $a_1 = 90$ and $a_2 = 360$

6. $a_1 = 16$ and $a_3 = 4$

_____

7. $a_1 = 2$ and $a_5 = 162$

8. $a_2 = 30$ and $a_3 = 10$

_____

9. $a_4 = 135$ and $a_5 = 405$

10. $a_3 = 400$ and $a_5 = 256$

_____

11. $a_2 = 80$ and $a_5 = 10$

12. $a_4 = 22$ and $a_7 = 0.022$

_____

A bank account earns a constant rate of interest each month. The account was opened on March 1 with $18,000 in it. On April 1, the balance in the account was $18,045. Use this information for Problems 13–15.

13. Write an explicit rule and a recursive rule that can be used to find $A(n)$, the balance after n months.

_____

14. Find the balance after 5 months.

_____

15. Find the balance after 5 years.

_____

Geometric Sequences
Reteach

In a **geometric sequence**, each term is *multiplied* by the same number
to get to the next term. This number is called the **common ratio**.

The common ratio is 4.

Determine if each sequence is a geometric sequence. Explain.

1. 2, 4, 6, 8, ... _____

2. −4, 8, −16, 32, ... _____

3. 32, 16, 8, 4, ... _____

You can write a geometric sequence using either a **recursive rule** or an **explicit rule**.

Recursive rule: Given $f(1)$, $f(n) = f(n-1) \cdot r$ for $n \geq 2$ Explicit rule: $f(n) = f(1) \cdot r^{n-1}$

Examples

Write a recursive rule and an explicit rule for the geometric sequence 1, 4, 16, 64, ...

Step 1.	Find the common ratio.	$r = 4$
Step 2.	Write a recursive rule.	$f(1) = 1$, $f(n) = f(n-1) \cdot 4$ for $n \geq 2$
Step 3.	Write an explicit rule.	$f(n) = 1 \cdot 4^{n-1}$

Each rule represents a geometric sequence. If the given rule is recursive, write it as an
explicit rule. If the rule is explicit, write it as a recursive rule. Assume that $f(1)$ is the first term
of the sequence. Write the first 4 terms of the sequence.

$f(1) = \dfrac{1}{4}$, $f(n) = f(n-1) \cdot 2$ for $n \geq 2$ $f(n) = 3 \cdot (2)^{n-1}$

Step 1. $f(n) = \dfrac{1}{4} \cdot 2^{n-1}$ Step 1. $f(1) = 3$, $f(n) = f(n-1) \cdot 2$ for $n \geq 2$

Step 2. $\dfrac{1}{4}, \dfrac{1}{2}, 1, 2, ...$ Step 2. 3, 6, 12, 24, ...

**Each rule represents a geometric sequence. If the given rule is
recursive, write it as an explicit rule. If the rule is explicit, write it as
a recursive rule. Assume that $f(1)$ is the first term of the sequence.**

4. $f(1) = 2$, $f(n) = f(n-1) \cdot 3$ for $n \geq 2$ 5. $f(n) = 5 \cdot (2)^{n-1}$

_____   _____

6. $f(n) = 1 \cdot (5)^{n-1}$ 7. $f(1) = \dfrac{1}{3}$, $f(n) = f(n-1) \cdot 3$ for $n \geq 2$

_____   _____

LESSON 10-4 Transforming Exponential Functions

Practice and Problem Solving: A/B

A parent function has equation $Y_1 = (0.25)^x$. For Problems 1–4, find the equation for Y_2.

1. Y_2 is a vertical stretch of Y_1. The values of Y_2 are 6 times those of Y_1.

   _____

2. Y_2 is a vertical shrink of Y_1. The values of Y_2 are half those of Y_1.

   _____

3. Y_2 is a translation of Y_1 4 units down.

   _____

4. Y_2 is a translation of Y_1 11 units up.

   _____

Values for $f(x)$, a parent function, and $g(x)$, a function in the same family, are shown below. Use the table for Problems 5–8.

x	−2	−1	0	1	2
f(x)	0.04	0.2	1	5	25
g(x)	0.016	0.08	0.4	2	10

5. Write equations for the two functions.

   _____

6. Is $g(x)$ a vertical stretch or a vertical shrink of $f(x)$? Explain how you can tell.

   _____

   _____

7. Do the graphs of $f(x)$ and $g(x)$ meet at any points? If so, find where. If not, explain why not?

   _____

   _____

8. Let $h(x)$ be the function defined by $h(x) = -f(x)$. Describe how the graph of $h(x)$ is related to the graph of $f(x)$.

   _____

   _____

LESSON 10-4 Transforming Exponential Functions
Reteach

The parent function for $f(x) = a(2)^x$ is $f(x) = 2^x$. When $a = 1$, the graph looks like this:

When a is greater than 1, the curve is steeper and has a higher y-intercept.

When a is between 0 and 1, the curve is less steep and has a lower y-intercept.

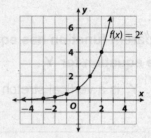

1. Compare the graph of $f(x) = 2^x$ and the graph of $f(x) = 3(2^x)$.
   Give the y-intercept for each graph.

   _____

2. Compare the graph of $f(x) = 2^x$ and the graph of $f(x) = 0.25(2^x)$.
   Give the y-intercept for each graph.

   _____

This graph compares $f(x) = a(4^x)$, when $a = 1$ and when $a = -1$:

When a is less than 0, the curve is reflected over the y-axis, so the curve is in Quadrants III and IV and has a negative y-intercept.

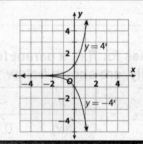

3. Compare the graph of $f(x) = 3(2^x)$ and the graph of $f(x) = -3(2^x)$.
   Give the y-intercept for each graph.

   _____

This graph compares $f(x) = 3^x$, $f(x) = 3^x + 5$, and $f(x) = 3^x - 5$:

For the function $f(x) = 3^x + c$, the curve has the same shape as for $f(x) = 3^x$ and it is translated up or down the y-axis by $(1 + c)$.

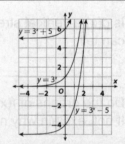

4. Compare the graph of $f(x) = 2^x$ and the graph of $f(x) = 2^x + 5$.
   Give the y-intercept for each graph.

   _____

5. Compare the graph of $f(x) = 2^x$ and the graph of $f(x) = 2^x - 3$.
   Give the y-intercept for each graph.

   _____

LESSON 10-5

Equations Involving Exponents

Practice and Problem Solving: A/B

Solve each equation without graphing.

1. $5^x = 625$

2. $\frac{1}{8}(2)^x = 32$

3. $\frac{2}{3}(3)^x = 162$

_____

_____

_____

4. $\frac{1}{12}(6)^x = 108$

5. $\left(\frac{4}{5}\right)^x = \frac{64}{125}$

6. $\frac{2}{3}\left(\frac{1}{2}\right)^x = \frac{1}{6}$

_____

_____

_____

7. $\frac{2}{5}(10)^x = 40$

8. $(0.1)^x = 0.00001$

9. $\frac{2}{3}\left(\frac{3}{8}\right)^x = \frac{9}{256}$

_____

_____

_____

Solve each equation by graphing. Round your answer to the nearest tenth. For each, write the equations of the functions you graphed first.

10. $9^x = 11$

Equation: _____

Equation: _____

Solution: _____

11. $12^x = 120$

Equation: _____

Equation: _____

Solution: _____

12. $6.2^x = 297$

Equation: _____

Equation: _____

Solution: _____

13. $0.5^x = 8.9$

Equation: _____

Equation: _____

Solution: _____

Solve. Round your answers to the nearest tenth.

14. A town with population of 600 is expected to grow at an annual rate of 5%. Write an equation and find the number of years it is expected to take the town to reach a population of 900.

_____

15. Find how long it will take $20,000 earning 3.5% annual interest to double in value.

_____

Name _____ Date _____ Class_____

LESSON 10-5

Equations Involving Exponents
Reteach

You can solve an equation with a variable exponent by writing both sides with the same base.

Example

Solve $25^3 = 5^x$.

$(5^2)^3 = 5^x$ Write 25 as a power of 5.
$5^6 = 5^x$ Use the properties of exponents to simplify.
$6 = x$ Since the bases are equal, the exponents are equal.

Solve each equation.

1. $4^x = 2^6$

   $x =$ _____

2. $3^x = 27^4$

   $x =$ _____

3. $2^x = \dfrac{1}{32}$

   $x =$ _____

You can solve an equation with a variable exponent by graphing both sides. The solution is the *x*-value at the point where the two graphs intersect.

You can use a calculator to find the point of intersection, or you can estimate from the graph.

Check your estimate with a calculator.

Example

Solve $3 = 2^x$ by graphing.

Write two equations: $y = 3$ and $y = 2^x$.
Graph both of the equations.
Find the *x*-value for the intersection.
$x \approx 1.6$
Check: Is $2^{1.6} \approx 3$?
Yes: $2^{1.6} = 3.0314\ldots$.

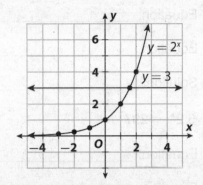

Solve each equation by graphing.

4. $5 = 2^x$

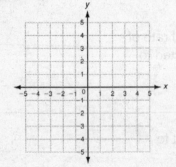

$x \approx$ _____

5. $3^x = 2$

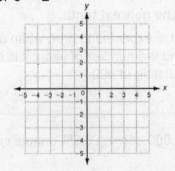

$x \approx$ _____

6. $3 = 4^x$

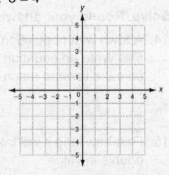

$x \approx$ _____

LESSON 11-1

Exponential Regression

Practice and Problem Solving: A/B

The table below shows the total attendance at major league baseball games, at 10-year intervals since 1930. Use the table for the problems that follow.

Major League Baseball Total Attendance (y_d), in millions, in years since 1930 (x)									
x	0	10	20	30	40	50	60	70	80
y_d	10.1	9.8	17.5	19.9	28.7	43.0	54.8	72.6	73.1
y_m									
residual									

1. Use a graphing calculator to find the exponential regression equation for this data. Round *a* and *b* to the nearest thousandth.

   _____

2. According to the regression equation, by what percent is attendance growing each year?

   _____

3. Complete the row labeled y_m above. This row contains the predicted *y*-values for each *x*-value. Round your answers to the nearest tenth.

4. Calculate the row of residuals above.

5. Analyze the residuals from your table. Does it seem like the equation is a good fit for the data?

   _____

   _____

6. Use your graphing calculator to find the correlation coefficient for the equation. Does the correlation coefficient make it seem like the equation is a good fit for the data?

   _____

   _____

7. Use the exponential regression equation to predict major league baseball attendance in 2020. Based on your earlier work on this page, do you think this is a reasonable prediction? Explain.

   _____

   _____

LESSON 11-1

Exponential Regression

Reteach

This table shows the number of computers sold at Computer Cave in the last six months.

Month	1	2	3	4	5	6
Number Sold	53	75	91	111	109	210

The owner wants to write a **regression equation** to model these sales. Then the owner will use the equation to predict future sales.

1. Enter this data into the calculator, putting the month (*x*) in List 1 and the number sold (*y*) in List 2.

   Graph the data as a scatter plot.
   Sketch the graph of these points.

2. Are the points in a straight line? _____

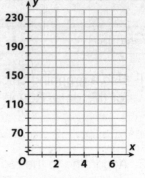

When the data do not fit a linear model, an exponential model may fit.

To find the exponential regression equation,
on the STAT menu select option 0 for exponential regression.

The computer screen shows you the values, *a* and *b*, for the exponential equation $y = ab^x$.

The screen also shows a value for *r*, the correlation coefficient.
When the value of *r*, the correlation coefficient, is close to 1, the equation is a good fit.

3. Write the values of *a*, *b*, and *r*, rounded to the hundredth.

   a = _____   *b* = _____   *r* = _____

4. Use these values to write the exponential equation. _____

5. Does this value of *r* indicate that the equation is a good fit, so it can predict future values fairly well? Explain.

   _____

6. Do the graph and the equation show that sales are increasing or decreasing? Explain.

   _____

7. Use the equation (and a calculator) to predict the number of sales for Month 8.

   _____

Comparing Linear and Exponential Models

LESSON
11-2

Practice and Problem Solving: A/B

Without graphing, tell whether each quantity is changing at a constant amount per unit interval, at a constant percent per unit interval, or neither. Justify your reasoning.

1. A bank account started with $1000 and earned $10 interest per month for two years. The bank then paid 2% interest on the account for the next two years.

   _____

2. Jin Lu earns a bonus for each sale she makes. She earns $100 for the first sale, $150 for the second sale, $200 for the third sale, and so on.

   _____

A bank offers annual rates of 6% simple interest or 5% compound interest on its savings accounts. Suppose you have $10,000 to invest. Use this information for Problems 3–8.

3. Express $f(x)$, the value of your deposit after x years in the simple interest account, and $g(x)$, the value of your deposit after x years in the compound interest account.

   _____

4. Is $f(x)$ or $g(x)$ a linear function? an exponential function? How can you tell?

   _____

   _____

5. Find the values of your deposit after three years in each account. Which account is the better choice?

   _____

6. Find the values of your deposit after 20 years in each account. Which account is the better choice?

   _____

7. Use a graphing calculator to determine the length of time an account must be held for the two choices to be equally attractive. Round your answer to the nearest tenth.

   _____

8. Use your answer to Problem 7 to write a statement that advises an investor regarding how to choose between the two accounts.

   _____

LESSON
11-2

Comparing Linear and Exponential Models
Reteach

Suppose you won a contest and had your choice of one of these two prizes—

Choice A: $50 for the first month and in each following month, $10 more than you got the month before.

Choice B: $50 for the first month and in each following month, 10% more than you got the month before.

Which would be the better choice?

Let m = the number of months after the first. Let p = amount paid in month m.

1. Complete the table.

	m	0	1	2	3	4	5	6
Choice A	p	50	$50 + 10(1) = 60$	$50 + 10(2) = 70$	80			
Choice B	p	50	$50 \times 1.10^1 = 55$	$50 \times 1.10^2 = 60.5$	66.55			

2. The prize only pays you for 6 months. Which is the better choice? Explain.

_____

With Choice A, you *add* a *fixed* amount ($10) each month. This is a **constant change**.
With Choice B, you *multiply* by 10% each month—finding 10% of an *increasing* amount. This is a **constant percent change**.
Choice A can be written as a **linear equation**.
Choice B can be written as an **exponential equation**.
What happens if the prize pays you for longer than 6 months? Is Choice A still the better choice? To find out, compare the equations for the two choices.

3. Write Choice A and Choice B as equations. _____

4. Use your equations to compare the amounts paid when $m = 11$.

   Choice A: _____   Choice B: _____

After a year, Choice A still pays more per month. To see if there is a month when Choice B will start to pay more each month, graph the equations and find the intersection.

5. Use this graph to estimate the value of m and p after which Choice B starts to pay more each month than Choice A.

   $m =$ _____ $p =$ _____

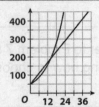

LESSON 12-1

Two-Way Frequency Tables

Practice and Problem Solving: A/B

Identify whether the survey question asks for numerical or categorical data.

1. How many children do you have?

   _____

2. What is your favorite movie?

   _____

3. For whom will you vote on Tuesday?

   _____

4. Do you know how to ride a bicycle?

   _____

Two students surveyed 50 students, each asking a different question. The two-way frequency tables show their findings. Complete each table.

5. Alia's Survey

Gender	Texts Received Daily, on Average			
	0	1–20	More than 20	Total
Boy	2	10		
Girl	1	7		25
Total				

6. Zach's survey

Gender	Favorite Potato			
	Baked	French Fries	Mashed	Total
Boy		10		26
Girl			12	
Total	8	18		

Use your completed tables to solve.

7. Did Alia and Zach survey the same number of girls as boys?

   _____

8. Did each student collect categorical or numerical data?

   _____

9. What percent of the students in the survey named baked potatoes as their favorite?

   _____

10. Did a greater fraction of girls or boys name mashed potatoes as their favorite? How can you tell?

    _____

    _____

11. Do you think any students in the survey do not have cellphones? Explain.

    _____

    _____

LESSON 12-1

Two-Way Frequency Tables
Reteach

Data collected in a table can be either **quantitative** or **qualitative**.

Quantitative Data	Can be expressed with numbers and measurements	weight, volume, distance, test scores, age, temperature
Qualitative or **Categorical** Data	Cannot be expressed with numbers	color, flavor, music type, kind of book, make of car

However, you can use numbers to count the **frequency** of qualitative data.

Example
This two-way frequency table shows the results of a survey of favorite subjects in school.

	English	Math	History	TOTAL
9th grade	8	12	4	**24**
10th grade	6	10	4	**?**
11th grade	12	8	6	**26**
TOTAL	**?**	**30**	**14**	**?**

How many 10th grade students were surveyed? $6 + 10 + 4 = 20$
How many students chose English? $8 + 6 + 12 = 26$
How many students were surveyed in all? $26 + 30 + 14 = 24 + 20 + 26 = 70$
How many more 9th graders than 11th graders chose Math? $12 - 8 = 4$

Identify whether the given data is categorical or quantitative.

1. closed, open   2. blue, brown, green   3. 7 ft, 13 ft, 2 ft

The table shows results for 100 people asked about films they saw.

4. Complete the table, and use it to complete the statements below.

Age:	Comedy	Adventure	Fantasy	TOTAL
under 20	33	9		**48**
20s		14	5	**27**
30s	15	7	3	
TOTAL	**56**			**100**

5. Were more than half of the people surveyed in the under-20 group?

   Explain. _____

6. Did each of the three groups see more comedy than they did

   adventure or fantasy? Explain. _____

Name _____ Date _____ Class_____

LESSON 12-2 Relative Frequency

Practice and Problem Solving: A/B

Tritt surveyed 125 people about their video watching habits. The two-way frequency table shows his findings. Use the data for Exercises 1–7.

| Age | How Often Do You Watch Video Online? | | | |
	Less than Once Each Week	Once or Twice Each Week	More than Twice Each Week	Total
Under 21	0	10	30	40
21–65	5	20	30	55
Over 65	20	6	4	30
Total	25	36	64	125

1. Create a two-way relative frequency table for the data. Round your decimals to the nearest hundredth.

| Age | How Often Do You Watch Video Online? | | | |
	Less than Once Each Week	Once or Twice Each Week	More than Twice Each Week	Total
Under 21				
21–65				
Over 65				
Total				

2. What percent of those surveyed were in each age group?

_____

3. What percent of those surveyed reported watching video online more than twice each week?

_____

Solve. Write your answers as percents. Round to the nearest whole percent, if necessary.

4. Find the conditional relative frequency that a person under 21 watches video online once or twice each week.

_____

5. Find the conditional relative frequency that a person who watches video online more than twice each week is over 65.

_____

6. Find the conditional relative frequency that a person who watches video online less than once each week is under 21.

_____

7. Find the conditional relative frequency that a person between the ages of 21 and 65 watches video online once or twice each week.

_____

LESSON 12-2

Relative Frequency
Reteach

This two-way frequency table shows the results of a survey of favorite subjects in school.

	English	Math	History	TOTAL
9th grade	8	12	4	24
10th grade	6	10	4	20
11th grade	12	8	6	26
TOTAL	26	30	14	70

To find the **joint relative frequency** of a category, divide the number in the cell by the grand total. For the first category, 9th grade English, this is $\frac{8}{70} = 0.11$.

To find the **marginal relative frequency**, divide the row or column total by the grand total. For the English column, this is $\frac{26}{70} = 0.37$

	English	Math	History	TOTAL
9th grade	$\frac{8}{70} = 0.11$	$\frac{12}{70} = 0.17$	$\frac{4}{70} = 0.06$	$\frac{24}{70} = 0.34$
10th grade	$\frac{6}{70} = 0.09$	$\frac{10}{70} = 0.14$	$\frac{4}{70} = 0.06$	$\frac{20}{70} = 0.29$
11th grade	$\frac{12}{70} = 0.17$	$\frac{8}{70} = 0.11$	$\frac{6}{70} = 0.09$	$\frac{26}{70} = 0.37$
TOTAL	$\frac{26}{70} = 0.37$	$\frac{30}{70} = 0.43$	$\frac{14}{70} = 0.20$	$\frac{70}{70} = 1$

	Soccer	Basketball	Baseball	TOTAL
Children	6	2	2	10
Teenagers	11	15	4	30
Adults	8	9	3	20
TOTAL	25	26	9	60

1. Use the data above to complete this two-way relative frequency table that shows how often sports are played. Round to two decimal places.

	Soccer	Basketball	Baseball	TOTAL
Children	$\frac{6}{60} = 0.10$	$\frac{2}{60} = 0.03$		
Teenagers				$\frac{30}{60} = 0.50$
Adults				
TOTAL		$\frac{26}{60} = 0.43$		

Name _____ Date _____ Class_____

LESSON
13-1

Find the mean, median, and range for each data set.

1. 18, 24, 26, 30

   Mean:_____

   Median: _____

   Range:_____

2. 5, 5, 9, 11, 13

   Mean:_____

   Median: _____

   Range: _____

3. 72, 91, 93, 89, 77, 82

   Mean:_____

   Median: _____

   Range: _____

4. 1.2, 0.4, 1.2, 2.4, 1.7, 1.6, 0.9, 1.0

   Mean: _____

   Median: _____

   Range: _____

The data sets below show the ages of the members of two clubs. Use the data for Problems 5–9.

   Club A: 42, 38, 40, 34, 35, 48, 38, 45
   Club B: 22, 44, 43, 63, 22, 27, 58, 65

5. Find the mean, median, range, and interquartile range for Club A.

   _____

6. Find the mean, median, range, and interquartile range for Club B.

   _____

7. Find the standard deviation for each club. Round to the nearest tenth.

   _____

8. Use your statistics to compare the ages and the spread of ages on the two clubs.

   _____

   _____

   _____

9. Members of Club A claim that they have the "younger" club. Members of Club B make the same claim. Explain how that could happen.

   _____

   _____

   _____

Name _____ Date _____ Class_____

LESSON	**Measures of Center and Spread**
13-1	*Reteach*

You can represent many values in a data set with just one central number. That central number may be the mean or the median.

Find the **mean** by adding the values and dividing by how many values are in the set.
Find the **median** by arranging the values in order and finding the middle value.

Example
For the data set 6, 10, 8, 13, 20, 9, 5
> Find the mean: $6 + 10 + 8 + 13 + 20 + 9 + 5 = 71$ and $71 \div 7 = 10.14$—the mean.
> Find the median: 5, 6, 8, **9**, 10, 13, 20. The middle number is 9—the median.

If a data set has two middle numbers,
the median is the average of those two, halfway between them.

With a graphing calculator you can find several statistics about a data set.

Example
Find statistics about this data set: 13, 25, 9, 11, 23, 8, 7, 2, 18, 23
Step 1: Use STAT and EDIT to enter the values into L_1. Check your entries for accuracy.
Step 2: Use STAT and CALC to see the 1-Var Stats by pressing ENTER twice.

$\bar{x} = 13.9$ $\bar{x}$ is the symbol for the **mean**. The mean is 13.9.

$\sum X = 139$ $\sum X$ is the symbol for the **sum of the values**. The sum is 139.

Skip down two to $\sigma x = 7.5$ *(rounded).* σx (say "sigma x") is the **standard deviation**.
- n = 10. n is the **number of values**. You entered 10 values.

- min$X$ = 2 tells you that the **minimum**, or lowest value, in the set is 2.
- Q_1 = 8 tells you that the **first quartile** is 8. Quartiles divide the set into 4 quarters.
- Med = 12 tells you that the **median**, or **second quartile**, is 12.
- Q_3 = 23 tells you that the **third quartile** is 23.

- max$X$ = 25 tells you that the **maximum**, or highest value, in the set is 25.
To find the **range**, find maximum − minimum. The range in this set is $25 - 2 = 23$.
To find the **interquartile range**, find $Q_3 - Q_1$. The interquartile range is $23 - 8 = 15$.

Range and standard deviation are measures of the **spread** of the data set.

Find each statistic for this data set: 5, 12, 22, 15, 17, 13, 25, 34, 7, 9

1. mean   2. median   3. range

_____   _____   _____

4. first quartile   5. interquartile range   6. standard deviation

_____   _____   _____

Original content Copyright © by Houghton Mifflin Harcourt. Additions and changes to the original content are the responsibility of the instructor.

84

Name _____ Date _____ Class_____

Data Distributions and Outliers

Practice and Problem Solving: A/B

For each data set, determine if 100 is an outlier. Explain why or why not.

1. 60, 68, 70, 78, 80, 82, 88

2. 70, 75, 77, 78, 80, 82, 88

_____

_____

The table below shows a major league baseball player's season home run totals for the first 14 years of his career. Use the data for Problems 3–8.

Season	1	2	3	4	5	6	7	8	9	10	11	12	13	14
Home Runs	18	22	21	28	30	29	32	40	33	34	28	29	22	20

3. Find the mean and median.

4. Find the range and interquartile range.

_____

_____

5. Make a line plot for the data.

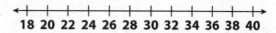

18 20 22 24 26 28 30 32 34 36 38 40

6. Examine the line plot. Do you think any of the season home run totals are outliers? Then test for any possible outliers.

_____

_____

7. Suppose the player begins his 15th season next week and you want to predict how many home runs he will hit this season. Does the table help you predict? Does the line plot help you predict? Explain your reasoning.

_____

_____

_____

8. Suppose the player hits 10 home runs in his 15th season. Which of the statistics from Problems 3 and 4 would change?

_____

_____

Data Distributions and Outliers

LESSON 13-2

Reteach

To make a **dot plot** from a data set, put an X above the number line for each value.

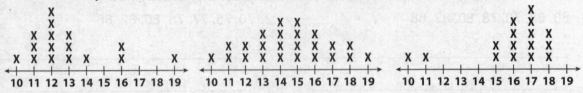

Skewed to the right   Symmetric   Skewed to the left

Find the **mean** of a data set; add the numbers and divide by the number of items in the set.

Find the **median**: list the items in order and find the middle number
(or the average of the two middle numbers).

Find the **range**: calculate maximum − minimum.

Find the **IQR** (the **interquartile range**): calculate $Q_3 - Q_1$ (quartile 3 minus quartile 1).

A data set may have an extreme value that does not fit in with the other values in the set. This **outlier** is sometimes removed from the data set because it distorts the central value.

A value, x, is an outlier if it is below $(Q_1 - \frac{3}{2}IQR)$ or above $(Q_3 + \frac{3}{2}IQR)$.

Example

Find the outliers in this data set: 2, 11, 14, 18, 21, 43

$Q_1 = 11$, $Q_3 = 21$, IQR = 10	1) Find Q_1, Q_3, and the IQR using a calculator.
$(Q_1 - \frac{3}{2}IQR) = 11 - 15 = -4$	2) Calculate $(Q_1 - \frac{3}{2}IQR)$ and $(Q_3 + \frac{3}{2}IQR)$
$(Q_3 + \frac{3}{2}IQR) = 21 + 15 = 36$	3) An outlier falls outside −4 to 36.
	43 is an outlier in this data set.

Use this data set to answer the questions below:
20, 25, 35, 40, 45, 50, 50, 55, 55, 55, 60, 60, 60, 65

1. Make a dot plot of the data. Identify the plot as symmetric, skewed left, or skewed right.

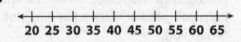

_____

2. Find the mean.   3. Find the median.   4. Find the IQR.

_____   _____   _____

5. If the number 100 were added to the data, would it be an outlier? Explain.

_____

6. Which of these would be changed by adding 90 to the data:
   mean, median, IQR? Explain.

_____

Histograms

Practice and Problem Solving: A/B

Solve each problem.

1. The number of calls per day to a fire and rescue service for three weeks is given below. Use the data to complete the frequency table.

Calls for Service
5 17 2 12 0   6   3   8 15 1 4
19 16 8 2   11 13 18 3 10 6

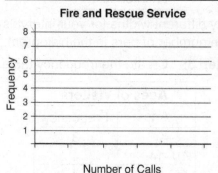

Fire and Rescue Service	
Number of Calls	**Frequency**
0–3	
4–7	
8–11	
12–15	
16–19	

2. Use the frequency table in Exercise 1 to make a histogram with a title and axis labels.

3. Which intervals have the same frequency?

_____

4. Is the distribution symmetrical? Explain.

_____

_____

5. Use the histogram to estimate the mean. Then compare your answer with the actual mean, found by using the original data.

_____

_____

6. Use the histogram to estimate the median. Then compare your answer with the actual median, found by using the original data.

_____

_____

7. By examining the histogram, can you tell that the mode number of calls lies in the first interval? Explain your reasoning.

_____

_____

LESSON 13-3

Histograms
Reteach

The ages of people visiting a water park during a certain time period
are given below. Use the data to make a frequency table with intervals.
Then make a histogram.

5, 12, 22, 15, 17, 13, 25, 34, 7, 9, 12, 32, 12, 15, 18

Step 1: Find the difference between the
greatest and least values.

Least: 5   Greatest: 34

$34 - 5 = 29$

Step 2: Use the difference to decide ⬜⇒
on intervals.

Try different widths for your intervals to determine
the number of bars in the histogram.

Step 3: Create the frequency table.

Finding the Interval		
If width of interval is:	Then divide:	The number of intervals is:
10	$\frac{29}{10} = 2.9$	3 (too few)
3	$\frac{29}{3} \approx 9.7$	10 (too many)
5	$\frac{29}{5} = 5.8$	6 (good)

Ages of Visitors	
Age	Frequency
5–9	3
10–14	4
15–19	4
20–24	1
25–29	1
30–34	2

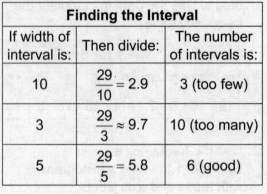

Step 4: Use the frequency table to create the histogram.
Draw each bar to the corresponding frequency.

1. The estimated miles per gallon for
selected cars are shown in the table.
Use the data to make a frequency table
with intervals. Then make a histogram.

Car Gas Mileage	
mi/gal	Frequency

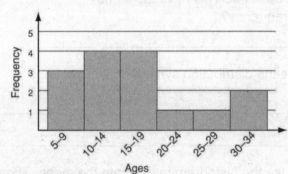

26	28	32	33	26	15	21
35	17	18	25	29	30	26
27	30	24	25	24	32	25
19	22	32	25	31	28	23
27	23	24	20	38	44	18

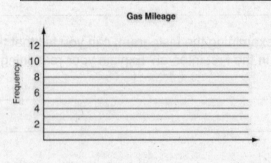

LESSON
13-4

Box Plots

Practice and Problem Solving: A/B

Use the box plot for Problems 1–3.

Daily Low Temperature

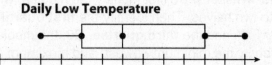

1. Find the median temperature.

2. Find the range.

_____

_____

3. Determine whether the temperature of 50° is an outlier.

_____

Weekly fuel economy figures for the drivers of two cars are shown in the box plots below. Use the box plots for Problems 4–8.

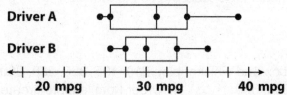

4. Who has the lowest overall weekly figure?

5. Who has the higher median?

_____

_____

6. Who has the lower interquartile range?

7. Who had the highest weekly figure?

_____

_____

8. The higher the number, the better the fuel economy. Based on the box plots, which driver has better overall fuel economy. Justify your conclusion.

_____

_____

_____

9. Make a box plot for this set of data. Be sure to mark the five key points.
   10, 14, 18, 12, 20, 24, 9, 25, 14, 16

Box Plots

LESSON 13-4

Reteach

Consider the data set {3, 5, 6, 8, 8, 10, 11, 13, 14, 19, 20}.

To make a **box-and-whisker plot**, first identify the median, which divides the data into two halves. Then identify the **first quartile**, Q1, the median of the lower half, and the **third quartile**, Q3, the median of the upper half. Last, identify the minimum (lowest) and maximum (greatest) numbers.

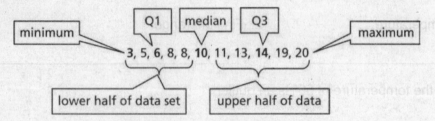

Plot the five numbers above a number line.
Draw a box so the sides go through Q1 and Q3.
Draw a line through the median. Connect the box to the minimum and maximum.

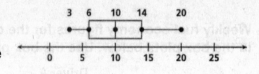

Example
Use this data to make a box-and-whisker plot: 210, 195, 350, 250, 260, 300

195, 210, 250, 260, 300, 350   1) Order from least to greatest.
      Q1   255   Q3
195, 210, 250, 260, 300, 350   2) Find the median, Q1 and Q3.

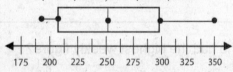

3) Graph on a number line. Mark the median.
4) Draw box from Q1 to Q3.
5) Connect box to maximum and minimum.

1. Write this data in order: 9, 11, 18, 21, 18, 14, 5 _____

2. Minimum: _____, Q1: ____, Median: ____, Q3: ____, Maximum: ____

3. Draw the box-and-whisker plot.

4. Write this data in order: 7, 5, 2, 14, 9, 15 _____

5. Minimum: _____, Q1: ____, Median: ____, Q3: ____, Maximum: ____

6. Draw the box-and-whisker plot.

LESSON 13-5

Normal Distributions

Practice and Problem Solving: A/B

A collection of data follows a normal distribution. Find the percent of the data that falls within the indicated range of the mean.

1. one standard deviation of the mean

   _____

2. three standard deviations of the mean

   _____

3. two standard deviations above the mean

   _____

4. one standard deviation below the mean

   _____

The amount of cereal in a carton is listed as 18 ounces. The cartons are filled by a machine, and the amount filled follows a normal distribution with mean of 18 ounces and standard deviation of 0.2 ounces. Use this information for Problems 5–7.

5. Find the probability that a carton of cereal contains less than its listed amount.

   _____

6. Find the probability that a carton of cereal contains between 18 ounces and 18.4 ounces.

   _____

7. Find the probability that a carton of cereal contains between 17.6 ounces and 18.2 ounces.

   _____

Suppose the manufacturer of the cereal above is concerned about your answer to Problem 5. A decision is made to leave the amount listed on the carton as 18 ounces while increasing the mean amount filled by the machine to 18.4 ounces. The standard deviation remains the same. Use this information for Problems 8–11.

8. Find the probability that a carton contains less than its listed amount.

   _____

9. Find the probability that a carton contains more than its listed amount.

   _____

10. Find the probability that a carton now contains more than 18.2 ounces.

    _____

11. Find the probability that a carton is more than 0.2 ounces underweight.

    _____

Normal Distributions

LESSON 13-5

Reteach

You can take a table of relative frequencies
showing measurement data, and
plot the frequencies as a histogram.
When the intervals for the histogram
are very small, the result is a special curve
called a **normal curve**, or **bell curve**.
Data that fits this curve is called normally distributed.
When you know the **median** (the *y*-height at 0)
and the **standard deviation** (marked as 1, 2, 3) of the data,
you can use the curve to draw conclusions and make predictions about the data.

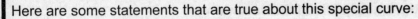

2.5% | 13.5% | 34% | 34% | 13.5% | 2.5%
−3 −2 −1 0 1 2 3
Standard Deviations

Here are some statements that are true about this special curve:

The mean and the median are the same—the center of the curve at its highest point.
The curve is symmetric. If you draw a vertical line at the median, the two sides match.
About 68% of all the data is within 1 standard deviation (−1 to +1) from the mean.
About 95% of all the data is within 2 standard deviations (−2 to +2) from the mean.
About 99.7% of all the data is within the 3 standard deviations (−3 to +3) from the mean.

Example

The scores for all the Algebra 1 students at Miller High on a test are
normally distributed with a mean of 82 and a standard deviation of 7.
What score is 1 standard deviation above the mean? 82 + 7 = **89**
What score is 1 standard deviation below the mean? 82 − 7 = **75**
What percent of students made scores between 75 and 89? **68%**
What percent of students made scores above 89? 13.5% + 2.5% = **16%**
What is the probability that a student made a score above 96? 82 + 2(7) = 96
This score is more than 2 standard deviations from the mean. The probability is **2.5%**

**The scores for all the 6th graders at Roberts School on a statewide
test are normally distributed with a mean of 76 and a standard
deviation of 10.**

1. What score is 1 standard deviation
   above the mean?

   _____

2. What score is 2 standard deviations
   below the mean?

   _____

3. What percent of the scores were
   below 66?

   _____

4. What percent of the scores were
   above 86?

   _____

5. What is the probability that a student made a score
   between 66 and 86?

   _____

LESSON 14-1 Understanding Polynomials
Practice and Problem Solving: A/B

Identify each expression as a monomial, a binomial, a trinomial or none of the above. Write the degree of each expression.

1. $6b^2 - 7$

   _____

2. $x^2y - 9x^4y^2 + 3xy$

   _____

3. $35r^3s$

   _____

4. $3p + \dfrac{2p}{q} - 5q$

   _____

5. $4ab^5 + 2ab - 3a^4b^3$

   _____

6. $st + t^{0.5}$

   _____

Simplify each expression.

7. $6n^3 - n^2 + 3n^4 + 5n^2$

   _____

8. $c^3 + c^2 + 2c - 3c^3 - c^2 - 4c$

   _____

9. $11b^2 + 3b - 1 - 2b^2 - 2b - 8$

   _____

10. $a^4b^3 + 9a^3b^4 - 3a^4b^3 - 4a^3b^4$

    _____

11. $9xy + 5x^2 + 15x - 10xy$

    _____

12. $3p^2q + 8p^3 - 2p^2q + 2p + 5p^3$

    _____

Determine the polynomial that has the greater value for the given value of *x*.

13. $4x^2 - 5x - 2$ or $5x^2 - 2x - 4$ for $x = 6$

    _____

14. $6x^3 - 4x^2 + 7$ or $7x^3 - 6x^2 + 4$ for $x = 3$

    _____

Solve.

15. A rocket is launched from the top of an 80-foot cliff with an initial velocity of 88 feet per second. The height of the rocket t seconds after launch is given by the equation $h = -16t^2 + 88t + 80$. How high will the rocket be after 2 seconds?

    _____

16. Antoine is making a banner in the shape of a triangle. He wants to line the banner with a decorative border. How long will the border be?

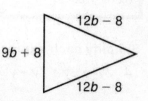

LESSON 14-1
Understanding Polynomials
Reteach

Polynomials have special names based on the number of terms.

Terms	1	2	3	4 or more
Name	Monomial	Binomial	Trinomial	Polynomial

The degree of a monomial is the sum of the exponents in the monomial. The degree of a polynomial is the degree of the term with the greatest degree.

Examples

Find the degree of $8x^2y^3$.

$8x^2y^3$ *The exponents are 2 and 3.*

The degree of the monomial is $2 + 3 = 5$.

Find the degree of $4ab + 9a^3$.

$\underset{2}{4ab} + \underset{3}{9a^3}$

Degree of the binomial is 3.

Identify each expression as a monomial, a binomial, a trinomial or none of the above. Write the degree of each expression.

1. $7m^3n^5$

2. $4x^2y^3 + y^4 + 7$

3. $x^5 - x^5y$

_____ _____ _____

You can simplify polynomials by combining like terms.

The following are like terms:

$4y$ and $7y$ $8x^2$ and $2x^2$ $7m^5$ and m^5

same variables raised to same power

The following are not like terms.

$3x^2$ and $3x$ $4y$ and 7 $8m$ and $3n$

same variable, different exponent   one with variable, one constant   same power, but different variable

Examples
Add $3x^2 + 4x + 5x^2 + 6x$.

$\underline{3x^2} + \underline{\underline{4x}} + \underline{5x^2} + \underline{\underline{6x}}$ *Identify like terms.*

$\underline{3x^2} + \underline{5x^2} + \underline{\underline{4x}} + \underline{\underline{6x}}$ *Rearrange terms so that like terms are together.*

$8x^2 + 10x$ *Combine like terms.*

Simplify each expression.

4. $2y^2 + 3y + 7y + y^2$

5. $8m^4 + 3m - 4m^4$

6. $12x^5 + 10x^4 + 8x^4$

_____ _____ _____

LESSON
14-2

Adding and Subtracting Polynomials

Practice and Problem Solving: A/B

Add or subtract.

1. $(10g^2 + 3g - 10) + (2g^2 + g + 9)$

_____

2. $(4x^3 - x^2 + 2x) + (3x^3 + x^2 + 4x)$

_____

3. $(11b^2 + 3b - 1) - (2b^2 + 2b + 8)$

_____

4. $(c^3 - c^2 + 2c) - (-3c^3 - c^2 - 4c)$

_____

5. $(ab^2 + 13b - 4a) + (3ab^2 + a + 7b)$

_____

6. $(9x^3 - 2x^2 + 3x) + (x^3 - x^2 - 3x)$

_____

7. $(-r^2 + 8pr - p) - (-12r^2 - 2pr + 8p)$

_____

8. $(mn - n^2 + 2mn^3) - (3mn^3 + n^2 + 4mn)$

_____

9. $(3y^2 - y + 3) + (2y^2 + 2y + 9)$

_____

10. $(4z^3 + 3z^2 + 8) + (2z^3 + z^2 - 3)$

_____

11. $(6s^3 + 9s + 10) - (3s^3 + 4s - 10)$

_____

12. $(15a^4 + 6a^2 + a) - (6a^4 - 2a^2 + a)$

_____

13. $(-7a^2b^3 + 3a^3b - 9ab) - (4a^2b^3 - 5a^3b + ab)$

_____

14. $(2p^4q^2 + 5p^3q - 2pq) + (8p^4q^2 - 3p^3q - pq)$

_____

Solve.

15. Darnell and Stephanie have competing refreshment stand businesses. Darnell's profit can be modeled with the polynomial $c^2 + 8c - 100$, where c is the number of items sold. Stephanie's profit can be modeled with the polynomial $2c^2 - 7c - 200$. Write a polynomial that represents the difference between Stephanie's profit and Darnell's profit.

_____

16. Write a polynomial to show how much Darnell and Stephanie can expect to earn if they decided to combine their businesses.

_____

17. A rectangular picture frame has the dimensions shown in the figure. Write a polynomial that represents the perimeter of the frame.

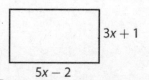

$3x + 1$

$5x - 2$

_____

LESSON 14-2
Adding and Subtracting Polynomials
Reteach

You can add or subtract polynomials by combining like terms.

Examples

Add $(5y^2 + 7y + 2) + (4y^2 + y + 8)$.

$(\underline{5y^2} + \underline{\underline{7y}} + \underline{\underline{\underline{2}}}) + (\underline{4y^2} + \underline{\underline{y}} + \underline{\underline{\underline{8}}})$ *Identify like terms.*

$(\underline{5y^2} + \underline{4y^2}) + (\underline{\underline{7y}} + \underline{\underline{y}}) + (\underline{\underline{\underline{2}}} + \underline{\underline{\underline{8}}})$ *Rearrange terms so that like terms are together.*

$\quad 9y^2 + 8y + 10$ *Combine like terms.*

Subtract $(6y^4 + 3y^2 - 7) - (2y^4 - y^2 + 5)$.

$(6y^4 + 3y^2 - 7) - (2y^4 - y^2 + 5)$

$(6y^4 + 3y^2 - 7) + (-2y^4 + y^2 - 5)$ *Rewrite subtraction as addition of the opposite.*

$(\underline{6y^4} + \underline{\underline{3y^2}} - \underline{\underline{\underline{7}}}) + (\underline{-2y^4} + \underline{\underline{y^2}} - \underline{\underline{\underline{5}}})$ *Identify like terms.*

$(\underline{6y^4} - \underline{2y^4}) + (\underline{\underline{3y^2}} + \underline{\underline{y^2}}) + (-\underline{\underline{\underline{7}}} - \underline{\underline{\underline{5}}})$ *Rearrange terms so that like terms are together.*

$\quad 4y^4 + 4y^2 - 12$ *Combine like terms.*

Add.

1. $(6x^2 + 3x) + (2x^2 + 6x)$ _____

2. $(m^2 - 10m + 5) + (8m + 2)$ _____

3. $(6x^3 + 5x) + (4x^3 + x^2 - 2x + 9)$ _____

4. $(2y^5 - 6y^3 + 1) + (y^5 + 8y^4 - 2y^3 - 1)$ _____

Subtract.

5. $(9x^3 - 5x) - (3x)$ _____

6. $(6t^4 + 3) - (-2t^4 + 2)$ _____

7. $(2x^3 + 4x - 2) - (4x^3 - 6)$ _____

8. $(t^3 - 2t) - (t^2 + 2t + 6)$ _____

9. $(4c^5 + 8c^2 - 2c - 2) - (c^3 - 2c + 5)$ _____

Multiplying Polynomials by Monomials
Practice and Problem Solving: A/B

Find the product.

1. $5x(2x^4y^3)$

   _____

2. $0.5p(-30p^3r^2)$

   _____

3. $11ab^2(2a^5b^4)$

   _____

4. $-6c^3d^5(-3c^2d)$

   _____

5. $4(3a^2 + 2a - 7)$

   _____

6. $9x^2(x^3 - 4x^2 - 3x)$

   _____

7. $6s^3(-2s^2 + 4s - 10)$

   _____

8. $5a^4(6a^4 - 2a^2 - a)$

   _____

9. $8pr(-7r^2 - 2pr + 8p)$

   _____

10. $2mn^3(3mn^3 + n^2 + 4mn)$

    _____

11. $-3x^4y^2(2x^2 + 5xy + 9y^2)$

    _____

12. $0.75\, v^2w^3(12v^3 + 16v^2w - 8w^2)$

    _____

13. $-7a^2b^3(4a^2b^3 + ab - 5a^3b)$

    _____

14. $2p^4q^2(8p^4q^2 - 3p^3q + 5p^2q)$

    _____

Solve.

15. The length of a rectangle is 3 inches greater than the width.

    a. Write a polynomial that represents the area
       of the rectangle.   _____

    b. Find the area of the rectangle when the
       width is 4 inches.   _____

16. The length of a rectangle is 8 centimeters less than 3 times the width.

    a. Write a polynomial that represents the area
       of the rectangle.   _____

    b. Find the area of the rectangle when the
       width is 10 centimeters.   _____

Name _____ Date _____ Class_____

LESSON 14-3
Multiplying Polynomials by Monomials
Reteach

To multiply monomials, multiply the constants, then multiply variables with the same base.

Example
Multiply $(3a^2b)(4ab^3)$.

$(3a^2b)(4ab^3)$

$(3 \bullet 4)(a^2 \bullet a)(b \bullet b^3)$ *Rearrange so that the constants and the variables with the same bases are together.*

$12a^3b^4$ *Multiply.*

To multiply a polynomial by a monomial, distribute the monomial to each term in the polynomial.

Example
Multiply $2x(x^2 + 3x + 7)$.

$2x(x^2 + 3x + 7)$

$(2x)x^2 + (2x)3x + (2x)7$ *Distribute.*

$2x^3 + 6x^2 + 14x$ *Multiply.*

Multiply.

1. $(-5x^2y^3)(2xy)$

2. $(2xyz)(-4x^2yz)$

3. $(3x)(x^2y^3)$

_____   _____   _____

Fill in the blanks below. Then finish multiplying.

4. $4(x - 5)$

$(\Box)x - (\Box)5$

5. $3x(x + 8)$

$(\Box)x + (\Box)8$

6. $2x(x^2 - 6x + 3)$

$(\Box)x^2 - (\Box)6x + (\Box)3$

_____   _____   _____

Multiply.

7. $5(x + 9)$

8. $-4x(x^2 + 8)$

9. $3x^2(2x^2 + 5x + 4)$

_____   _____   _____

10. $-3(5 - x^2 + 2)$

11. $(5a^3b)(2ab)$

12. $5y(-y^2 + 7y - 2)$

_____   _____   _____

LESSON 14-4

Multiplying Polynomials
Practice and Problem Solving: A/B

Multiply.

1. $(x + 5)(x + 6)$

2. $(a - 7)(a - 3)$

3. $(d + 8)(d - 4)$

4. $(2x - 3)(x + 4)$

5. $(5b + 1)(b - 2)$

6. $(3p - 2)(2p + 3)$

7. $(5k - 9)(2k - 4)$

8. $(2m - 5)(3m + 8)$

9. $(4 + 7g)(5 - 8g)$

10. $(r + 2s)(r - 6s)$

11. $(3 - 2v)(2 - 5v)$

12. $(5 + h)(5 - h)$

13. $(y + 3)(y - 3)$

14. $(z - 5)^2$

15. $(3q + 7)(3q - 7)$

16. $(4w + 9)^2$

17. $(3a - 4)^2$

18. $(5q - 8r)(5q + 8r)$

19. $(x + 4)(x^2 + 3x + 5)$

20. $(3m + 4)(m^2 - 3m + 5)$

21. $(2x - 5)(4x^2 - 3x + 1)$

Solve.

22. Write a polynomial that represents the area of the trapezoid. $\left(A = \frac{1}{2}h(b_1 + b_2)\right)$

6x − 5 / x + 1 / 4x + 7

23. If $x = 4$ in., find the area of the trapezoid in problem 22.

24. Kayla worked $3x + 6$ hours this week. She earns $x - 2$ dollars per hour. Write a polynomial that represents the amount Kayla earned this week. Then calculate her pay for the week if $x = 11$.

LESSON 14-4

Multiplying Polynomials
Reteach

Use the Distributive Property to multiply binomials and polynomials.

Examples

Multiply $(x + 3)(x - 7)$.

$(x + 3)(x - 7)$

$x(x - 7) + 3(x - 7)$ *Distribute.*

$(x)x - (x)7 + (3)x - (3)7$ *Distribute again.*

$x^2 - \underline{7x} + \underline{3x} - 21$ *Multiply.*

$x^2 - 4x - 21$ *Combine like terms.*

Multiply $(x + 5)(x^2 + 3x + 4)$.

$(x + 5)(x^2 + 3x + 4)$

$x(x^2 + 3x + 4) + 5(x^2 + 3x + 4)$ *Distribute.*

$(x)x^2 + (x)3x + (x)4 + (5)x^2 + (5)3x + (5)4$ *Distribute again.*

$x^3 + \underline{3x^2} + \underline{4x} + \underline{5x^2} + \underline{15x} + 20$ *Multiply.*

$x^3 + 8x^2 + 19x + 20$ *Combine like terms.*

Fill in the blanks below. Then finish multiplying.

1. $(x + 4)(x - 5)$

$\square(x - 5) + \square(x - 5)$

_____

2. $(x - 2)(x + 8)$

$\square(x + 8) - \square(x + 8)$

_____

3. $(x - 3)(x - 6)$

$\square(x - 6) - \square(x - 6)$

_____

Multiply.

4. $(x - 2)(x - 3)$

_____

5. $(x - 7)(x + 7)$

_____

6. $(x + 2)(x + 1)$

_____

Fill in the blanks below. Then finish multiplying.

7. $(x + 3)(2x^2 + 4x + 8)$

$\square(2x^2 + 4x + 8) + \square(2x^2 + 4x + 8)$

_____

8. $(x + 2)(6x^2 + 4x + 5)$

$\square(6x^2 + 4x + 5) + \square(6x^2 + 4x + 5)$

_____

LESSON 15-1 Factoring Polynomials

Practice and Problem Solving: A/B

Find the GCF of each pair of monomials.

1. $15x^4$ and $35x^2$ _____

2. $12p^2$ and $30q^5$ _____

3. $-6t^3$ and $9t$ _____

4. $27y^3z$ and $45x^2y$ _____

5. $12ab$ and 12 _____

6. $-8d^3$ and $14d^4$ _____

Factor each polynomial. Check your answer.

7. $8c^2 + 7c$

8. $3n^3 + 12n^2$

9. $15x^5 - 18x$

_____ _____ _____

10. $-8s^4 + 20t^3 - 28$

11. $6n^6 + 18n^4 - 24n$

12. $-5m^4 - 5m^3 + 5m^2$

_____ _____ _____

Factor each expression.

13. $3m(m + 5) + 4(m + 5)$

14. $16b(b - 3) + (b - 3)$

_____ _____

Factor each polynomial by grouping.

15. $2x^3 + 8x^2 + 3x + 12$

16. $4n^3 + 3n^2 + 4n + 3$

_____ _____

17. $10d^2 - 6d + 35d - 21$

18. $12n^3 - 15n^2 - 8n + 10$

_____ _____

19. $5b^4 - 15b^3 + 3 - b$

20. $t^3 - 5t^2 + 10 - 2t$

_____ _____

LESSON
15-1

Factoring Polynomials
Reteach

Factor $12x^3 + 21x^2 + 15x$.

Step 1: Find the GCF of all the terms in the polynomial.

The factors of $12x^3$ are: 1, 2, **3**, 4, 6, 12, **x**, x, x.

The factors of $21x^2$ are: 1, **3**, 7, 21, **x**, x. } The GCF is **3x.**

The factors of $15x$ are: 1, **3**, 5, 15, **x**.

Step 2: Write terms as products using the GCF.

$12x^3 + 21x^2 + 15x$

$(3x)4x^2 + (3x)7x + (3x)5$

Step 3: Use the Distributive Property to factor out the GCF.

$3x(4x^2 + 7x + 5)$

Factor each polynomial.

1. $20x^2 - 15x$ 2. $44a^2 + 11a$ 3. $24y - 36x$

_____   _____   _____

When a polynomial has four terms, make two groups and factor out the GCF from each group.

Factor $8x^3 + 6x^2 + 20x + 15$.

Step 1: Group terms that have common factors.

$$(8x^3 + 6x^2) + (20x + 15)$$

Step 2: Identify and factor the GCF out of each group.

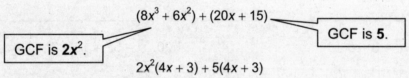

$$(8x^3 + 6x^2) + (20x + 15)$$

GCF is **2x².**   GCF is **5**.

$$2x^2(4x + 3) + 5(4x + 3)$$

Step 3: Factor out the common binomial factor.

$$2x^2(4x + 3) + 5(4x + 3)$$

GCF is $(4x + 3)$. $(4x + 3)(2x^2 + 5)$

Factor each polynomial by grouping.

4. $21x^3 + 12x^2 + 14x + 8$ 5. $40x^3 - 50x^2 + 12x - 15$

_____   _____

LESSON 15-2

Factoring $x^2 + bx + c$

Practice and Problem Solving: A/B

Factor each trinomial.

1. $x^2 + 7x + 10$ 2. $x^2 + 9x + 8$ 3. $x^2 + 13x + 36$

_____ _____ _____

4. $x^2 + 9x + 14$ 5. $x^2 + 7x + 12$ 6. $x^2 + 9x + 18$

_____ _____ _____

7. $x^2 - 9x + 18$ 8. $x^2 - 5x + 4$ 9. $x^2 - 9x + 20$

_____ _____ _____

10. $x^2 - 12x + 20$ 11. $x^2 - 11x + 18$ 12. $x^2 - 12x + 32$

_____ _____ _____

13. $x^2 + 7x - 18$ 14. $x^2 + 10x - 24$ 15. $x^2 + 2x - 3$

_____ _____ _____

16. $x^2 + 2x - 15$ 17. $x^2 + 5x - 6$ 18. $x^2 + 5x - 24$

_____ _____ _____

19. $x^2 - 5x - 6$ 20. $x^2 - 2x - 35$ 21. $x^2 - 7x - 30$

_____ _____ _____

22. $x^2 - x - 56$ 23. $x^2 - 2x - 8$ 24. $x^2 - x - 20$

_____ _____ _____

25. Factor $n^2 + 5n - 24$. Show that the original polynomial and the factored form describe the same sequence of numbers for $n = 0, 1, 2, 3,$ and 4.

_____

n	$n^2 + 5n - 24$		n	

LESSON 15-2

Factoring $x^2 + bx + c$
Reteach

When factoring $x^2 + bx + c$:

If c is positive	and b is positive	both factors are positive.
	and b is negative	both factors are negative.

$$x^2 + 7x + 10$$

Need factors of **10** that sum to **7**.

Factors of 10	Sum
1 and 10	11 ✗
2 and 5	7 ✓

$(x + 2)(x + 5)$

$$x^2 - 9x + 18$$

Need factors of **18** that sum to **−9**.

Factors of 18	Sum
−1 and −18	−19 ✗
−2 and −9	−11 ✗
−3 and −6	−9 ✓

$(x - 3)(x - 6)$

Factor each trinomial.

1. $x^2 + 13x + 12$

2. $x^2 + 15x + 50$

3. $x^2 - 13x + 36$

_____   _____   _____

When factoring $x^2 + bx + c$:

If c is negative	and b is positive	the larger factor must be positive.
	and b is negative	the larger factor must be negative.

$$x^2 + 8x - 20$$

Need factors of **−20** that sum to **8**.
(Make larger factor positive.)

Factors of −20	Sum
−1 and 20	19 ✗
−2 and 10	8 ✓
−4 and 5	1 ✗

$(x - 2)(x + 10)$

$$x^2 - 3x - 28$$

Need factors of **−28** that sum to **−3**.
(Make larger factor negative.)

Factors of 18	Sum
1 and −28	−27 ✗
2 and −14	−12 ✗
4 and −7	−3 ✓

$(x + 4)(x - 7)$

Factor each trinomial.

4. $x^2 + 3x - 18$

5. $x^2 - 5x - 14$

6. $x^2 + 4x - 45$

_____   _____   _____

**LESSON
15-3**

Factoring $ax^2 + bx + c$

Practice and Problem Solving: A/B

Factor each trinomial.

1. $2x^2 + 13x + 15$

   _____

2. $3x^2 + 10x + 8$

   _____

3. $4x^2 + 24x + 27$

   _____

4. $5x^2 + 21x + 4$

   _____

5. $4x^2 + 11x + 7$

   _____

6. $6x^2 - 23x + 20$

   _____

7. $7x^2 - 59x + 24$

   _____

8. $3x^2 - 14x + 15$

   _____

9. $8x^2 - 73x + 9$

   _____

10. $2x^2 + 11x - 13$

    _____

11. $9x^2 + 6x - 48$

    _____

12. $2x^2 + 17x - 30$

    _____

13. $8x^2 + 29x - 12$

    _____

14. $11x^2 + 25x - 24$

    _____

15. $18x^2 - 6x - 8$

    _____

16. $12x^2 - 7x - 12$

    _____

17. $9x^2 - 49x - 30$

    _____

18. $6x^2 + x - 40$

    _____

19. $-12x^2 - 35x - 18$

    _____

20. $-20x^2 + 29x - 6$

    _____

21. $-2x^2 + 5x + 42$

    _____

22. The area of a rectangle is $20x^2 - 27x - 8$.

    The length is $4x + 1$. What is the width? _____

LESSON 15-3
Factoring $ax^2 + bx + c$
Reteach

When factoring $ax^2 + bx + c$, first find factors of a and c. Then check the products of the inner and outer terms to see if the sum is b.

$2x^2 + 11x + 15 = (\blacksquare x + \blacksquare)(\blacksquare x + \blacksquare)$ $3x^2 - 23x + 14 = (\blacksquare x + \blacksquare)(\blacksquare x + \blacksquare)$

Factors of 2	Factors of 15	Outer + Inner
1 and 2	1 and 15	$1 \cdot 15 + 2 \cdot 1 = 17$ ✗
1 and 2	15 and 1	$1 \cdot 1 + 2 \cdot 15 = 31$ ✗
1 and 2	5 and 3	$1 \cdot 3 + 2 \cdot 5 = 13$ ✗
1 and 2	3 and 5	$1 \cdot 5 + 2 \cdot 3 = 11$ ✓

$(x + 3)(2x + 5)$

Factors of 3	Factors of 14	Outer + Inner
1 and 3	−1 and −14	$1 \cdot (-14) + 3 \cdot (-1) = -17$ ✗
1 and 3	−14 and −1	$1 \cdot (-1) + 3 \cdot (-14) = -43$ ✗
1 and 3	−2 and −7	$1 \cdot (-7) + 3 \cdot (-2) = -13$ ✗
1 and 3	−7 and −2	$1 \cdot (-2) + 3 \cdot (-7) = -23$ ✓

$(x - 7)(3x - 2)$

When c is negative, one factor of c is positive and one is negative. You can stop checking factors when you find the factors that work.

$2x^2 + 7x - 15 = (\blacksquare x + \blacksquare)(\blacksquare x + \blacksquare)$

Factors of 2	Factors of −15	Outer + Inner
1 and 2	−3 and 5	$1 \cdot 5 + 2 \cdot (-3) = -1$ ✗
1 and 2	3 and −5	$1 \cdot (-5) + 2 \cdot 3 = 1$ ✗
1 and 2	−5 and 3	$1 \cdot 3 + 2 \cdot (-5) = -7$ ✗
1 and 2	5 and −3	$1 \cdot (-3) + 2 \cdot 5 = 7$ ✓

$(x + 5)(2x - 3)$

Factor each trinomial.

1. $3x^2 + 7x + 4$

2. $2x^2 - 13x + 21$

3. $4x^2 + 8x + 3$

_____   _____   _____

4. $3x^2 - 7x - 20$

5. $5x^2 + 34x - 7$

6. $7x^2 - 11x - 6$

_____   _____   _____

LESSON
15-4
Factoring Special Products
Practice and Problem Solving: A/B

Determine whether each trinomial is a perfect square. If so, factor it. If not, explain why.

1. $x^2 + 6x + 9$

_____

2. $4x^2 + 20x + 25$

_____

3. $36x^2 - 24x + 16$

_____

4. $9x^2 - 12x + 4$

_____

5. A square fountain in the center of a shopping mall
has an area of $(4x^2 + 12x + 9)$ ft^2. The dimensions of the
fountain are of the form $cx + d$, where c and d are whole
numbers. Find an expression for the perimeter of the
fountain. Find the perimeter when $x = 2$ ft.

_____

**Determine whether each binomial is the difference of perfect squares.
If so, factor it. If not, explain why.**

6. $x^2 - 16$

_____

7. $9b^4 - 200$

_____

8. $1 - m^6$

_____

9. $36s^2 - 4t^2$

_____

10. $x^2y^2 + 196$

_____

LESSON 15-4
Factoring Special Products
Reteach

If a polynomial is a perfect square trinomial, the polynomial can be factored using a pattern.

$$a^2 + 2ab + b^2 = (a + b)^2$$
$$a^2 - 2ab + b^2 = (a - b)^2$$

Determine whether $4x^2 + 20x + 25$ is a perfect square trinomial. If so, factor it. If not, explain why.

Step 1: Find a, b, then $2ab$.

$a = \sqrt{4x^2} = 2x$ *The first term is a perfect square.*

$b = \sqrt{25} = 5$ *The last term is a perfect square.*

$2ab = 2(2x)(5) = 20x$ *Middle term (20x) = 2ab.*

Therefore, $4x^2 + 20x + 25$ is a perfect square trinomial.

Step 2: Substitute expressions for a and b into $(a + b)^2$.

$$(2x + 5)^2$$

Factor.

1. $x^2 - 14x + 49$ 2. $16x^2 + 24x + 9$ 3. $9x^2 - 60x + 100$

_____   _____   _____

If a binomial is a difference of perfect squares, it can be factored using a pattern.

$$a^2 - b^2 = (a + b)(a - b)$$

Determine whether $64x^2 - 25$ is a difference of perfect squares. If so, factor it. If not, explain why.

Step 1: Determine if the binomial is a difference.

$64x^2 - 25$ *The minus sign indicates it is a difference.*

Step 2: Find a and b.

$a = \sqrt{64x^2} = 8x$ *The first term is a perfect square.*

$b = \sqrt{25} = 5$ *The last term is a perfect square.*

Therefore, $64x^2 - 25$ is a difference of perfect squares.

Step 3: Substitute expressions for a and b into $(a + b)(a - b)$.

$$(8x + 5)(8x - 5)$$

Factor.

4. $x^2 - 36$ 5. $4x^2 - 81$ 6. $9x^2 - 100$

_____   _____   _____

LESSON 16-1 Solving Quadratic Equations Using Square Roots
Practice and Problem Solving: A/B

Simplify fully.

1. $\sqrt{169}$

2. $\sqrt{\dfrac{4}{25}}$

3. $-\sqrt{400}$

_____   _____   _____

4. $-\sqrt{576}$

5. $\sqrt{\dfrac{144}{81}}$

6. $-\sqrt{90,000}$

_____   _____   _____

Solve.

7. $x^2 - 121 = 0$

8. $x^2 - 49 = 0$

9. $x^2 - 16 = 20$

_____   _____   _____

10. $(x - 3)^2 = 0$

11. $(x + 2)^2 + 1 = 10$

12. $(x - 8)^2 - 5 = 31$

_____   _____   _____

13. $(x + 5)^2 - 6 = 43$

14. $x^2 - 19 = 81$

15. $(x - 14)^2 + 13 = 14$

_____   _____   _____

16. $(x + 10)^2 + 1 = 65$

17. $12 - (x - 2)^2 = 3$

18. $100 - (x + 5)^2 = 64$

_____   _____   _____

Solve.

19. An auditorium has a floor area of 20,000 square feet. The length of the auditorium is twice its width. Find the dimensions of the room.

_____

20. A ball is dropped from a height of 64 feet. Its height, in feet, can be modeled by the function $h(t) = -16t^2 + 64$, where t is the time in seconds since it is dropped.

(a) Find how long it takes the ball to reach the ground.

_____

(b) Find how long it takes the ball to fall 36 feet. (Hint: first find its height.)

_____

LESSON 16-1 Solving Quadratic Equations Using Square Roots
Reteach

If a quadratic equation is in the form $x^2 = a$, where a is a positive number, you can take the square root of both sides to find the solutions. Remember to find both the positive and negative square roots.

Examples

Solve $x^2 = 144$ using square roots.

$x^2 = 144$
$x = \pm\sqrt{144}$
$x = \pm 12$

The solutions are −12 and 12.

Solve $x^2 - 36 = 0$ using square roots.

$x^2 - 36 = 0$
$x^2 = 36$ 　　　Add 36 to both sides.
$x = \pm\sqrt{36}$
$x = \pm 6$

The solutions are −6 and 6.

Solve $(x - 2)^2 = 25$ using square roots.

$(x - 2)^2 = 25$
$x - 2 = \pm\sqrt{25}$ 　　　Take the square root of both sides.
$x = \pm 5 + 2$ 　　　Add 2 to both sides.
$x = -5 + 2$ or $x = 5 + 2$ 　　　Solve for both cases.
$x = -3$ 　　　 $x = 7$

The solutions are −3 and 7.

Solve using square roots.

1. $x^2 = 9$

2. $x^2 = 16$

3. $x^2 = 1$

_____

_____

_____

4. $x^2 - 400 = 0$

5. $x^2 - 49 = 0$

6. $x^2 - 64 = 0$

_____

_____

_____

7. $(x - 6)^2 = 144$

8. $(x + 5)^2 = 81$

9. $(x - 4)^2 = 100$

_____

_____

_____

10. $(x + 3)^2 = 121$

11. $(x - 1)^2 = 36$

12. $(x + 2)^2 = 4$

_____

_____

_____

LESSON 16-2

Solving $x^2 + bx + c = 0$ by Factoring

Practice and Problem Solving: A/B

Find the zeros of each function.

1. $f(x) = (x - 3)(x + 5)$

   _____

2. $f(x) = x^2 - x$

   _____

3. $f(x) = x^2 + 2x + 1$

   _____

4. $f(x) = x^2 - 4x - 5$

   _____

Solve by factoring.

5. $x^2 - 3x = 0$

   _____

6. $x^2 + 4x + 3 = 0$

   _____

7. $x^2 + 5x - 6 = 0$

   _____

8. $x^2 + 11x + 24 = 0$

   _____

9. $x^2 - 12x + 11 = 0$

   _____

10. $x^2 + 18x + 65 = 0$

   _____

11. $x^2 = 3x + 40$

   _____

12. $x^2 - 14 = 5x$

   _____

13. $x^2 = 5x$

   _____

14. $x^2 = 9x - 18$

   _____

15. $2x^2 + 10x - 28 = 0$

   _____

16. $x^2 + 3 = 6x - 5$

   _____

17. $5x^2 + 10x = 75$

   _____

18. $9x^2 = 10x$

   _____

19. $2x^2 + 4x = 12 + x^2$

   _____

Solve.

20. The product of two consecutive integers is 72. Find all solutions.

   _____

21. The length of a rectangle is 8 feet more than its width. The area of the
    rectangle is 84 square feet. Find its length and width.

   _____

22. The height of a flare fired from the deck of a ship in distress can be
    modeled by $h = -16t^2 + 80t + 96$, where h is the height of the flare
    above water in feet and t is the time in seconds. Find the number of
    seconds it takes the flare to hit the water.

   _____

LESSON 16-2

Solving $x^2 + bx + c = 0$ by Factoring

Reteach

Quadratic Equations can be solved by factoring and using the Zero Product Property.

If the product of two quantities equals zero, at least one of the quantities must equal zero.

If $(x)(y) = 0$, then   If $(x + 3)(x - 2) = 0$, then

$x = 0$ or $y = 0$ $x + 3 = 0$ or $x - 2 = 0$

You can use the Zero Product Property to solve any quadratic equation written in standard form, $x^2 + bx + c = 0$, provided the quadratic expression is factorable.

Examples

Find the zeros of $f(x) = x^2 + 4x - 5$.

$f(x) = x^2 + 4x - 5$
$x^2 + 4x - 5 = 0$ *Set f(x) equal to 0.*
$(x + 5)(x - 1) = 0$ *Factor $x^2 + 4x - 5$.*
$x + 5 = 0$ or $x - 1 = 0$ *Set each factor equal to 0.*
$x = -5$ or $x = 1$ *Solve each equation for x.*

Solve $x^2 - 5x = 14$.

$x^2 - 5x = 14$
$x^2 - 5x - 14 = 0$ *Write the equation in standard form.*
$(x - 7)(x + 2) = 0$ *Factor $x^2 - 5x - 14$.*
$x - 7 = 0$ or $x + 2 = 0$ *Set each factor equal to 0.*
$x = 7$ or $x = -2$ *Solve each equation for x.*

Use the Zero Product Property to solve each equation by filling in the boxes below. Then find the solutions. Check your answer.

1. $(x - 6)(x - 3) = 0$

$\boxed{} = 0$ or $\boxed{} = 0$

2. $(x + 8)(x - 5) = 0$

$\boxed{} = 0$ or $\boxed{} = 0$

Find the zeros.

3. $f(x) = x^2 + x - 12$

4. $f(y) = y^2 - 10y + 21$

5. $f(n) = n^2 - 2n - 15$

Solve.

6. $t^2 + 6t = 27$

7. $x^2 - 9x = -18$

8. $a^2 - 7a = 30$

LESSON 16-3

Solving $ax^2 + bx + c = 0$ by Factoring

Practice and Problem Solving: A/B

Solve the equations by factoring.

1. $2x^2 - 3x = 2x - 2$

2. $3x^2 - 4x = 6x - 3$

3. $3x^2 - 7x = x - 4$

4. $5x^2 + 6x = -5x - 2$

5. $4x^2 + 16x - 48 = 0$

6. $2x^2 - 32 = 0$

7. $2x^2 - 7 = 14 - 11x$

8. $7x^2 - 12x = 36 + 7x$

9. $5x^2 = 45$

10. $2x^2 - 7x = 15 - 6x$

11. $4x^2 - 20x = -25$

12. $5x^2 - 20x + 20 = 0$

13. $3x^2 + 5x = 6 - 2x$

14. $2x^2 + 3x + 6 = 4x$

15. $3x^2 = 9x$

16. $9x^2 - 13x = 8x - 10$

17. $4x^2 - 50x + 49 = 50x$

18. $4x^2 + 21x = 6x - 14$

19. $24x^2 - x = 10x - 1$

20. $3x^2 + 12x - 15 = 0$

Solve.

21. The height of a flare fired from the deck of a ship in distress can be modeled by $h = -16t^2 + 104t + 56$, where h is the height in feet of the flare above water and t is the time in seconds. Find the time it takes

the flare to hit the water._____

LESSON 16-3

Solving $ax^2 + bx + c = 0$ by Factoring

Reteach

When a factorable quadratic expression is written in standard form, $ax^2 + bx + c = 0$, you can use the Zero Product Property to solve the equation.

To solve a quadratic equation, move all terms to the left side of the equation to get 0 on the right side.

Example

Solve $3x^2 + 4x = 8 - 6x$ by factoring.

$3x^2 + 4x = 8 - 6x$

$3x^2 + 4x + 6x - 8 = 0$ *Subtract 8 and add 6x to both sides.*

$3x^2 + 10x - 8 = 0$ *Simplify.*

$(3x - 2)(x + 4) = 0$ *Factor the quadratic expression.*

$3x - 2 = 0$ or $x + 4 = 0$ *Set each factor equal to 0.*

$x = \dfrac{2}{3}$ or $x = -4$ *Solve each equation.*

Sometimes you can factor out a common factor.

Example

Solve $3x^2 - 12x + 12 = 0$ by factoring.

$3x^2 - 12x + 12 = 0$

$3(x^2 - 4x + 4) = 0$ *Factor out a common factor.*

$3(x - 2)(x - 2) = 0$ *Factor the quadratic expression.*

Set each factor equal to 0.

$3 \neq 0$ or $x - 2 = 0$ *Solve each equation.*

$x = 2$

Use the Zero Product Property to find the solutions.

1. $(2x - 3)(x + 9) = 0$

2. $(5x - 1)(x + 2) = 0$

3. $2(3x - 1)(3x - 1) = 0$

Solve the equations by factoring.

4. $2x^2 + 5x + 3 = -2x$

5. $6x^2 - 3x = 2 - 4x$

6. $7x^2 + 8x = -10x - 11$

7. $18x^2 + 24x + 8 = 0$

8. $10x^2 - 25x - 15 = 0$

9. $6x^2 = 96$

LESSON 16-4

Solving $x^2 + bx + c = 0$ by Completing the Square

Practice and Problem Solving: A/B

Complete the square to form a perfect square trinomial.

1. $x^2 + 4x +$ ☐

2. $x^2 - 16x +$ ☐

3. $x^2 + 7x +$ ☐

Solve each equation by completing the square.

4. $x + 6x = -8$

5. $x^2 + 4x = 12$

6. $x^2 - 2x = 15$

_____   _____   _____

7. $x^2 + 8x = 48$

8. $x^2 + 6x = 27$

9. $x^2 - 2x = 35$

_____   _____   _____

10. $x^2 - 2x = 24$

11. $x^2 - 6x = -5$

12. $x^2 + 10x = -16$

_____   _____   _____

13. $x^2 - 3x = 28$

14. $x^2 - 2x = 63$

15. $x^2 + 5x = 50$

_____   _____   _____

16. $x^2 - x = 56$

17. $x^2 - 9x = 36$

18. $x^2 + 13x = -30$

_____   _____   _____

Solve.

19. A rectangular deck has an area of 320 ft^2. The length of the deck is
    4 feet longer than the width. Find the dimensions of the deck. Solve by
    completing the square.

_____

LESSON 16-4
Solving $x^2 + bx + c = 0$ by Completing the Square
Reteach

To solve a quadratic equation in the form $x^2 + bx = c$, first complete the square of $x^2 + bx$. Then solve using square roots.

Solve $x^2 + 10x = -24$ by completing the square.

Step 1: Write equation in form $x^2 + bx = c$. Identify *b*.

$x^2 + 10x = -24$

Step 4: Factor the perfect square trinomial on the left.

$x^2 + 10x + 25 = 1$

$(x + 5)^2 = 1$

Step 2: Find $\left(\dfrac{b}{2}\right)^2$.

$\left(\dfrac{10}{2}\right)^2 = 5^2 = 25$

Step 5: Take the square root of both sides.

$\sqrt{(x + 5)^2} = \pm\sqrt{1}$

$x + 5 = \pm 1$

Step 3: Add $\left(\dfrac{b}{2}\right)^2$ to both sides.

$x^2 + 10x = -24$

$ +25 +25$

$x^2 + 10x + 25 = 1$

Step 6: Write and solve two equations.

$x + 5 = 1$ OR $x + 5 = -1$

$ -5 -5$ $ -5 -5$

$x = -4$ OR $x = -6$

The solutions are -4 and -6.

Solve by completing the square.

1. $x^2 - 6x = 7$

2. $x^2 + 8x = -12$

3. $x^2 - 2x = 63$

_____ _____ _____

4. $x^2 + 4x = 32$

5. $x^2 - 14x = -24$

6. $x^2 + 12x = -13$

_____ _____ _____

LESSON 16-5

Solving $ax^2 + bx + c = 0$ by Completing the Square

Practice and Problem Solving: A/B

Complete the square to form a perfect square trinomial.

1. $4x^2 + 8x + \boxed{}$

2. $16x^2 - 24x + \boxed{}$

3. $25x^2 - 10x + \boxed{}$

_____   _____   _____

Solve each equation by completing the square.

4. $4x^2 + 8x = 10$

5. $16x^2 - 24x = 2$

6. $25x^2 - 10x = 8$

_____   _____   _____

7. $-x^2 + 2x = -24$

8. $49x^2 + 28x = 22$

9. $9x^2 - 12x = 35$

_____   _____   _____

10. $8x^2 + 4x = 4$

11. $18x^2 - 6x = 15$

12. $10x^2 + 2x = 5$

_____   _____   _____

13. $3x^2 - 6x = 11$

14. $2x^2 - 6x = -4$

15. $64x^2 + 16x = -1$

_____   _____   _____

Solve

16. A small painting has an area of 400 cm^2. The length is 4 more than 2 times the width. Find the dimensions of the painting. Solve by completing the square. Round answers to the nearest tenth of a centimeter.

_____

LESSON 16-5 Solving $ax^2 + bx + c = 0$ by Completing the Square
Reteach

To solve a quadratic equation in the form $ax^2 + bx = c$, first divide both sides of the equation by a, so the coefficient of x^2 will be 1. Then solve by completing the square.

Solve $4x^2 + 16x = 40$.

Step 1: Divide both sides of the equation by a.
$4x^2 + 16x = 40$
$x^2 + 4x = 10$

Step 2: Find $\left(\dfrac{b}{2}\right)^2$.

$\left(\dfrac{4}{2}\right)^2 = 2^2 = 4$

Step 3: Add $\left(\dfrac{b}{2}\right)^2$ to both sides.

$x^2 + 4x + 4 = 10 + 4$

$x^2 + 4x + 4 = 14$

Step 4: Factor the perfect square trinomial on the left.
$(x + 2)^2 = 14$

Step 5: Take the square root of both sides.
$x + 2 = \pm\sqrt{14}$

Step 6: Find the solutions.
$x = -2 \pm\sqrt{14}$

Solve by completing the square.

1. $5x^2 + 40x = 25$

2. $2x^2 - 24x = -4$

3. $3x^2 - 24x = 9$

4. $9x^2 - 18x = 27$

5. $4x^2 - 16x = -12$

6. $16x^2 + 32x = 64$

7. $25x^2 + 100x = 75$

8. $9x^2 - 36x = 54$

9. $4x^2 + 24x = 20$

LESSON 16-6 **The Quadratic Formula**

Practice and Problem Solving: A/B

Solve using the quadratic formula.

1. $x^2 + x = 12$

2. $4x^2 - 17x - 15 = 0$

_____   _____

3. $2x^2 - 5x = 3$

4. $3x^2 + 11x + 5 = 0$

_____   _____

Find the number of real solutions of each equation using the discriminant.

5. $x^2 + 25 = 0$

6. $x^2 - 11x + 28 = 0$

7. $x^2 + 8x + 16 = 0$

_____   _____   _____

Solve using any method.

8. $x^2 + 8x + 15 = 0$

9. $x^2 - 49 = 0$

_____   _____

10. $6x^2 + x - 1 = 0$

11. $x^2 + 8x - 20 = 0$

_____   _____

12. In the past, professional baseball was played at the Astrodome in Houston, Texas. The Astrodome has a maximum height of 63.4 m. The height in meters of a baseball t seconds after it is hit straight up in the air with a velocity of 45 m/s is given by $h = -9.8t^2 + 45t + 1$. Will a baseball hit straight up with this velocity hit the roof of the Astrodome? Use the discriminant to explain your answer.

_____

_____

LESSON 16-6

The Quadratic Formula

Reteach

The Quadratic Formula can be used to solve any quadratic equation.

$$x = \frac{-b \pm \sqrt{b^2 - 4ac}}{2a}$$

Solve $2x^2 - 5x - 12 = 0$ using the quadratic formula.

$$2x^2 - 5x - 12 = 0$$

Step 1: Identify a, b, and c.

$a = 2$

$b = -5$

$c = -12$

Step 2: Substitute into the quadratic formula.

$$x = \frac{-(-5) \pm \sqrt{(-5)^2 - 4(2)(-12)}}{2(2)}$$

Step 3: Simplify.

$$x = \frac{-(-5) \pm \sqrt{(-5)^2 - 4(2)(-12)}}{2(2)}$$

$$x = \frac{5 \pm \sqrt{25 - (-96)}}{4}$$

$$x = \frac{5 \pm \sqrt{121}}{4}$$

$$x = \frac{5 \pm 11}{4}$$

Step 4: Write two equations and solve.

$$x = \frac{5 + 11}{4} \quad \text{or} \quad x = \frac{5 - 11}{4}$$

$$x = 4 \quad \text{or} \quad x = -\frac{3}{2}$$

Solve using the quadratic formula by filling in the blanks below.

1. $x^2 + 2x - 35 = 0$

   $a = $ ____; $b = $ ____; $c = $ ____

   $$x = \frac{-(\boxed{}) \pm \sqrt{(\boxed{})^2 - 4(\boxed{})(\boxed{})}}{2\boxed{}}$$

   Simplify:

   _____

2. $3x^2 + 7x + 2 = 0$

   $a = $ ____; $b = $ ____; $c = $ ____

   $$x = \frac{-(\boxed{}) \pm \sqrt{(\boxed{})^2 - 4(\boxed{})(\boxed{})}}{2\boxed{}}$$

   Simplify:

   _____

3. $x^2 + x - 20 = 0$

   $a = $ ____; $b = $ ____; $c = $ ____

   $$x = \frac{-(\boxed{}) \pm \sqrt{(\boxed{})^2 - 4(\boxed{})(\boxed{})}}{2\boxed{}}$$

   Simplify:

   _____

4. $2x^2 - 9x - 5 = 0$

   $a = $ ____; $b = $ ____; $c = $ ____

   $$x = \frac{-(\boxed{}) \pm \sqrt{(\boxed{})^2 - 4(\boxed{})(\boxed{})}}{2\boxed{}}$$

   Simplify:

   _____

Translating Quadratic Functions
Practice and Problem Solving: A/B

Find the domain, range, and vertex of each function.

1. $f(x) = x^2 + 8$

_____

_____

_____

2. $f(x) = (x - 4)^2 - 6$

_____

_____

_____

3. $f(x) = (x + 2)^2 - 1$

_____

_____

_____

4. $f(x) = (x - 11)^2 + 7$

_____

_____

_____

5. $f(x) = (x - 12)^2$

_____

_____

_____

6. $f(x) = (x + 10)^2 + 5$

_____

_____

_____

Use the function $f(x) = x^2$ to write the equation of each new function, $g(x)$.

7. The graph of $f(x)$ is translated 2 units up.

_____

8. The graph of $f(x)$ is translated 5 units to the left and 3 units down.

_____

9. The graph of $f(x)$ is translated 8 units to the right.

_____

10. The graph of $f(x)$ is translated 4 units down and 6 units to the right.

_____

The price of admission to an amusement park, in dollars, is modeled by the equation $f(x) = (x - 2010)^2 + 48$, where x is the year. Use this model for Problems 11–12.

11. What were the prices of admission in 2010, 2011, and 2012?

_____

12. Do you think the model makes sense for years before 2010? Explain.

_____

_____

LESSON 17-1
Translating Quadratic Functions
Reteach

The graph of the parent quadratic function can be translated
to make the graph of a related function.

Parent Function and Graph	Translation Up	Translation Down	Translation Right	Translation Left
$f(x) = x^2$	$f(x) = x^2 + k, k > 0$	$f(x) = x^2 + k, k < 0$	$f(x) = (x - h)^2, h > 0$	$f(x) = (x - h)^2, h < 0$
Domain: all reals Range: $y \geq 0$	$f(x) = x^2 + 2$ Domain: all reals Range: $y \geq 2$	$f(x) = x^2 - 2$ Domain: all reals Range: $y \geq -2$	$f(x) = (x - 2)^2$ Domain: all reals Range: $y \geq 0$	$f(x) = (x + 2)^2$ Domain: all reals Range: $y \geq 0$

Graph each quadratic equation and give the domain and range.

1. $f(x) = x^2 + 3$

Domain: _____

Range: _____

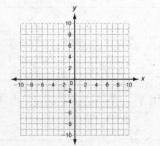

2. $f(x) = (x - 3)^2$

Domain: _____

Range: _____

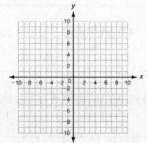

3. $f(x) = (x + 3)^2$

Domain: _____

Range: _____

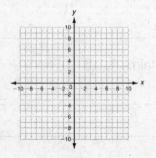

4. $f(x) = x^2 - 3$

Domain: _____

Range: _____

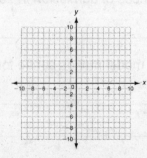

LESSON
17-2

Stretching, Shrinking, and Reflecting Quadratic Functions
Practice and Problem Solving: A/B

Order the functions from narrowest to widest.

1. $f(x) = x^2$; $g(x) = 5x^2$; $h(x) = -\dfrac{4}{5}x^2$

2. $f(x) = \dfrac{2}{9}x^2$; $g(x) = -x^2$; $h(x) = -\dfrac{3}{2}x^2$

_____   _____

Use a table of values to graph each quadratic function.

3. $y = -\dfrac{1}{2}x^2$

x	–4	–2	0	2	4
y					

4. $y = 4x^2$

x	–2	–1	0	1	2
y					

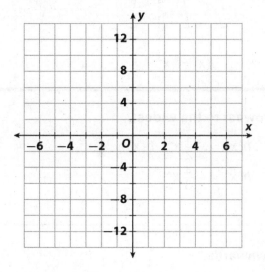

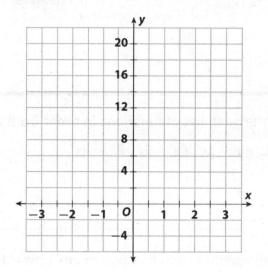

Write the equation for each quadratic function.

5. The parabola to the right

_____

6. Vertex at (0, 0) and contains the point (1, 13)

_____

7. Vertex at (0, 0) and contains the point (3, –6)

_____

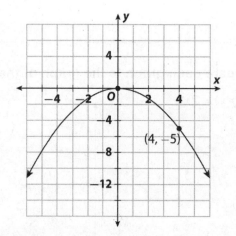

8. Vertex at (0, 0) and contains the point $\left(\dfrac{1}{2}, \dfrac{1}{2}\right)$

_____

Name _____ Date _____ Class _____

**LESSON
17-2**

Stretching, Shrinking, and Reflecting Quadratic Functions
Reteach

The graph of $f(x) = ax^2$ will become narrower (shrinks) or wider (stretches) compared to the graph of the parent function $f(x) = x^2$.

If $|a| < 1$	Graph is wider
If $|a| > 1$	Graph is narrower

If $a < 0$, then the graph opens downward: The parent graph is reflected over the y-axis.

As the absolute value of a gets smaller, the graph gets wider.

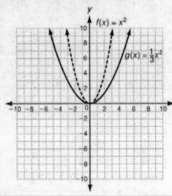

$g(x)$ is wider than $f(x)$.

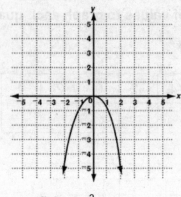

$f(x) = -x^2$

Write each list of functions in order from the narrowest to the widest.

1. $f(x) = 3x^2$, $f(x) = 6x^2$, $f(x) = 2x^2$

2. $h(x) = -\frac{1}{2}x^2$, $h(x) = \frac{3}{4}x^2$, $h(x) = -\frac{4}{3}x^2$

_____   _____

Tell whether each function opens upwards or downwards.

3. $f(x) = 9x^2$ 4. $f(x) = -3x^2$ 5. $f(x) = \frac{1}{2}x^2$

_____   _____   _____

Compare each graph to the graph of the parent function $f(x) = x^2$.

6. $g(x) = 2x^2$

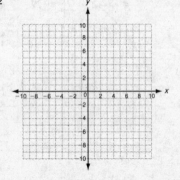

7. $h(x) = -\frac{1}{2}x^2$

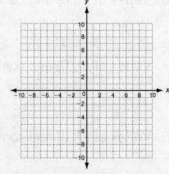

_____   _____

LESSON 17-3

Combining Transformations of Quadratic Functions

Practice and Problem Solving: A/B

For each quadratic function, identify the vertex and whether its graph opens up or down.

1. $f(x) = 3(x - 2)^2 + 11$

2. $f(x) = -(x + 1)^2$

_____   _____

3. $f(x) = \frac{3}{4}(x + 9)^2 - 1$

4. $f(x) = -4(x - 5)^2 - 3$

_____   _____

Match each quadratic function with the letter corresponding to its graph shown below.

5. $y = 0.5x^2 + 2$ _____

6. $y = 2(x + 4)^2 - 2$ _____

7. $y = x^2 + 2$ _____

8. $y = 2(x - 4)^2 - 2$ _____

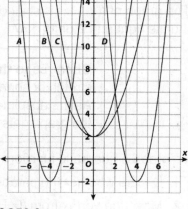

Two balls are dropped at the same time, one from a height of 250 feet and the other from 400 feet. Use this information for Problems 9–10.

9. Write the two height functions, $h_1(t)$ and $h_2(t)$, where t = seconds.

_____

10. Find the heights of the balls three seconds after they are released.

_____

Solve.

11. Write the equation of the function whose graph is the result of shifting the graph of $y = 3x^2$ two units to the left and five units down.

_____

12. Write the equation of the function whose graph is the result of shifting the graph of $y = -2x^2$ three units up and four units to the right.

_____

LESSON 17-3

Combining Transformations of Quadratic Functions
Reteach

The graph of a quadratic function is a parabola.
   The parent function is $f(x) = x^2$.

Quadratic function $f(x) = a(x - h)^2 + k$.

Use the graph of $f(x) = x^2$ to help you graph quadratic functions.

Changes to *h* and *k* move the parent graph right or left or up or down.
These translations change the vertex (0, 0) of the parent graph.

Parent Function	Transformation
$f(x) = x^2$	$g(x) = (x - h)^2 + k$
Vertex: (0, 0)	Vertex: (h, k)

The translation shifts $f(x) = x^2$:
h units right ($h > 0$) or left ($h < 0$) and
k units up ($k > 0$) or down ($k < 0$)

The vertex of $g(x) = (x - 4)^2 - 2$ is (4, –2)

The graph of $f(x) = x^2$ is shifted
4 units right and 2 units down.

Changes to the value of *a*
stretch or shrink the graph.
As the absolute value of *a* gets smaller,
the graph gets wider.

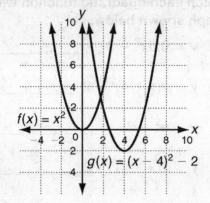

To graph a quadratic function:

1. Decide whether the parabola opens up ($a > 0$) or down ($a < 0$).

2. Move the vertex from (0, 0) using the values of *h* and *k*.

3. Stretch or shrink the parent graph using the value of *a*.

4. Make a table of values to find other points.

Graph each quadratic function.

1. $h(x) = -5(x + 1)^2 + 4$

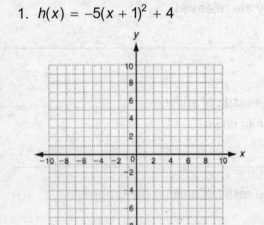

2. $g(x) = \frac{1}{2}(x - 2)^2 - 3$

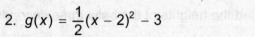
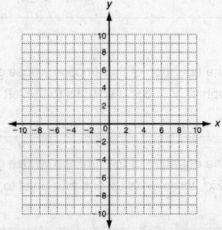

LESSON 17-4 Characteristics of Quadratic Functions
Practice and Problem Solving: A/B

Determine whether each function is quadratic or not.

1. $y = x^2 + 3x + 2x^3$

   _____

2. $3y + x^2 = 6 - x$

   _____

3. $x^2 - 9 = x + y + 3x^2$

   _____

4. $y^2 = x^2 + 1$

   _____

Determine the characteristics of each quadratic function.

5. $y = 2(x + 3)^2 - 2$

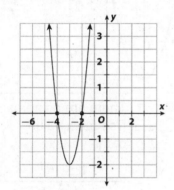

6. $y = -\dfrac{1}{2}(x - 1)^2 - 1$

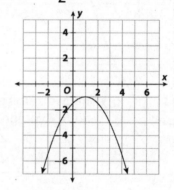

Vertex: _____

Minimum (if any): _____

Maximum (if any): _____

Range: _____

Zeros (if any): _____

Axis of symmetry: _____

Vertex: _____

Minimum (if any): _____

Maximum (if any): _____

Range: _____

Zeros (if any): _____

Axis of symmetry: _____

Solve.

7. A quadratic function has zeros of –2 and 14. Find its axis of symmetry.

   _____

8. The axis of symmetry of a quadratic function has equation $x = 4$. If one of the function's zeros is 7, what must the other zero be?

   _____

Name _____ Date _____ Class_____

LESSON 17-4

Characteristics of Quadratic Functions
Reteach

When $y = 0$, the graph of a quadratic function intercepts the x-axis.

These x-intercepts are called the **zeros**, or solutions, of the equation.

A quadratic function may have two, one, or no zeros.

When the graph only touches the x-axis, there is only one zero. $x = -1$

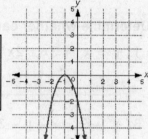

You find the **axis of symmetry** of a parabola by averaging the two zeros. If there is only one zero or no zeros, use the x-value of the vertex.

Find the axis of symmetry of each parabola.

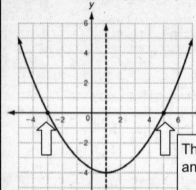

The two zeros are −3 and 5. Average the zeros:

$$\frac{-3+5}{2} = \frac{2}{2} = \boxed{1}$$

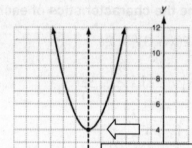

There are no zeros. Use the x-value of the vertex:

$(\boxed{-6}, 4)$

The axis of symmetry is $x = 1$.

The axis of symmetry is $x = -6$.

At the **vertex**, the y-value is a **minimum** ($a > 0$) or **maximum** ($a < 0$).

The minimum is $f(x) = -4$.

The minimum is $f(x) = 4$.

1. Which does this graph have, a maximum or a minimum? _____

2. What is the maximum or minimum value for this function? _____

3. What are the zeros of this function?

_____

4. What is the axis of symmetry of this function?

_____

5. What is the vertex of this function?

_____

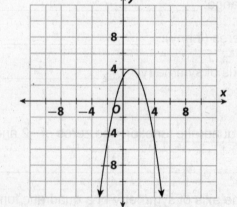

Name _____ Date _____ Class_____

LESSON 17-5

Solving Quadratic Equations Graphically
Practice and Problem Solving: A/B

Solve each equation graphically.

1. $x^2 - 5 = -1$

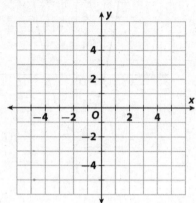

_____

2. $(x - 2)^2 + 1 = 5$

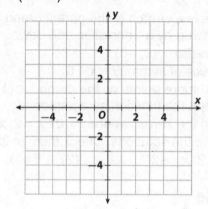

_____

3. $-0.25x^2 + 4 = 3$

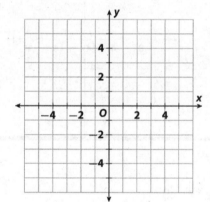

_____

4. $-2(x + 1)^2 + 5 = 3$

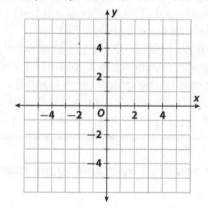

_____

An object is dropped from 300 feet above the ground. Its height (in feet) is modeled by the function $h(t) = -16t^2 + 300$, where t is the seconds since being dropped. Use this information for Problems 5–6.

5. Find the height of the object 2.5 seconds after being dropped.

_____

6. Suppose the object hits the top of a tree that is 44 feet above the ground. Write and solve an equation that allows you to find how many seconds after being dropped that this occurs.

_____

LESSON 17-5 — Solving Quadratic Equations Graphically

Reteach

To solve $2x^2 - 8 = 0$ by graphing the related function, use these steps.

1. Rewrite $2x^2 - 8 = 0$ as the related function.
   $y = 2x^2 - 8$
2. This is a stretch of the parent graph $y = x^2$
   followed by a translation of 8 down.
   vertex = $(0, -8)$
   axis of symmetry: $x = 0$.
3. Find more points on the graph. $(1, -6)$, $(-1, -6)$
4. Graph the function as a parabola.
5. Find the zeros (where $y = 0$): $x = 2$; $x = -2$
6. Write the solutions. Check them in $2x^2 - 8 = 0$.
   $x = 2$; $x = -2$ $2(2)^2 - 8 = 0$; $2(-2)^2 - 8 = 0$

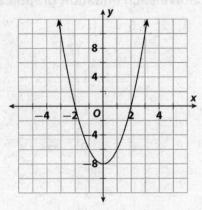

Example

Solve $-(x - 1)^2 + 4 = 0$ by graphing.

Rewrite as $y = -(x - 1)^2 + 4$.
Since $a = -1$, the parabola opens downward.
The parent graph is translated to the right 1
    and up 4. The vertex is at $(1, 4)$
The axis of symmetry is $x = 1$.
Find more points: $(0, 3)$, $(2, 3)$ and graph.
The graph crosses the x-axis at -1 and 3.
The zeros of the graph are -1 and 3.
The solutions of $-(x - 1)^2 + 4 = 0$ are $x = -1$ and $x = 3$.
Check: $-((-1) - 1)^2 + 4 = 0$ and $-(3 - 1)^2 + 4 = 0$

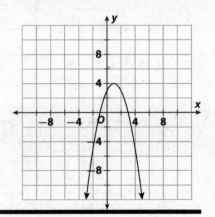

Solve each equation by graphing the related function.

1. $3x^2 - 3 = 0$

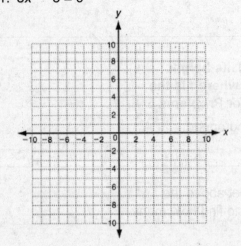

2. $0 = (x + 1)^2 - 9$

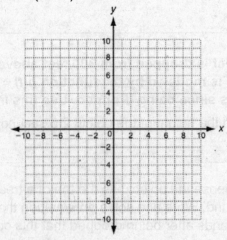

_____   _____

LESSON 17-6

Solving Systems of Linear and Quadratic Equations

Practice and Problem Solving: A/B

Solve each system represented by the functions graphically.

1. $\begin{cases} y = x^2 - 2 \\ y = 5x - 8 \end{cases}$

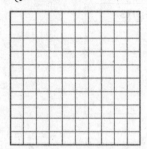

2. $\begin{cases} y = x^2 - 4x + 6 \\ y = -x + 4 \end{cases}$

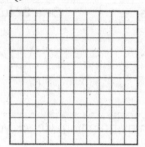

_____   _____

Solve each system algebraically.

3. $\begin{cases} y = x^2 - 3 \\ y = -x + 3 \end{cases}$

4. $\begin{cases} y = x^2 - 2x - 3 \\ y = -2x - 5 \end{cases}$

_____   _____

5. $\begin{cases} y = 2x^2 + x - 3 \\ -3x + y = 1 \end{cases}$

6. $\begin{cases} y = x^2 - 25 \\ y = x + 5 \end{cases}$

_____   _____

7. $\begin{cases} y = x^2 - 1 \\ 2x - y = -2 \end{cases}$

8. $\begin{cases} y = x^2 + 4x + 3 \\ x - y = -1 \end{cases}$

_____   _____

Solve.

9. A ball is thrown upward with an initial velocity of 40 feet per second from ground level. The height of the ball, in feet, after t seconds is given by $h = -16t^2 + 40t$. At the same time, a balloon is rising at a constant rate of 10 feet per second. Its height, in feet, after t seconds is given by $h = 10t$. Find the time it takes for the ball and the balloon to reach the same height.

_____

LESSON 17-6

Solving Systems of Linear and Quadratic Equations
Reteach

A *nonlinear system of equations* is a system in which at least one of the equations is nonlinear.

Possible Solutions for a Linear-Quadratic System

No Solutions	One Solution	Two Solutions
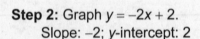		

Solve the system by graphing. Check your answer.

$$\begin{cases} y = x^2 - 3x - 4 \\ y = -2x + 2 \end{cases}$$

Step 1: Graph $y = x^2 - 3x - 4$.
   Axis of symmetry: $x = 1.5$; vertex: $(1.5, -6.25)$
   y-intercept: $(0, -4)$; another point $(-2, 6)$
   Graph the points and reflect them across the axis of symmetry.

Step 2: Graph $y = -2x + 2$.
   Slope: -2; y-intercept: 2

Step 3: Find the points of intersection: $(-2, 6)$ and $(3, -4)$.

Check: Substitute the solutions into each system.

$(-2, 6)$	$(3, -4)$
$y = x^2 - 3x - 4$	$y = x^2 - 3x - 4$
$6 = (-2)^2 - 3(-2) - 4$	$-4 = 3^2 - 3(3) - 4$
$6 = 6 ✓$	$-4 = -4 ✓$
$y = -2x + 2$	$y = -2x + 2$
$6 = -2(-2) + 2$	$-4 = -2(3) + 2$
$6 = 6 ✓$	$-4 = -4 ✓$

Solve each system by graphing. Check your answers.

1. $\begin{cases} y = x^2 + 3x - 4 \\ y = 4x - 4 \end{cases}$

2. $\begin{cases} y = 3x^2 + 2x - 1 \\ y = 2x + 2 \end{cases}$

LESSON 17-7 Comparing Linear, Quadratic, and Exponential Models

Practice and Problem Solving: A/B

Determine if each function is linear, quadratic, exponential, or none of these.

1. $f(x) = -\dfrac{1}{4}x^2 + 9$

_____

2. $f(x) = 17x - 12$

_____

3. $f(x) = -3^x + 1$

_____

4. $f(x) = x^2 + 2^x$

_____

5. $(1, 4), (2, 8), (3, 16), (4, 32), (5, 64)$

_____

6. $(-2, 10), (0, 5), (2, 0), (4, -5), (6, -10)$

_____

7. $(0, 1), (1, 5), (2, 25), (3, 75), (4, 225)$

_____

8. $(-2, -3), (-1, 6), (0, 9), (1, 6), (2, -3)$

_____

Determine the end behavior for $f(x)$ as x approaches infinity.

9. $f(x) = -4^{x+1}$

_____

10. $f(x) = \dfrac{1}{100}x^2 - 10{,}000$

_____

11. $f(x) = 10x + 9$

_____

12. $f(x) = -3x^2 + 500$

_____

Todd had a piggy bank holding $384. He began taking out money each month. The table shows the amount remaining, in dollars, after each of the first four months. Use the table for Problems 13–14.

Month	0	1	2	3	4
Amount	384	192	96	48	24

13. Does the data follow a linear, quadratic, or exponential model? How can you tell?

_____

_____

14. How much will be left in the piggy bank at the end of the fifth month?

_____

LESSON 17-7
Comparing Linear, Quadratic, and Exponential Models
Reteach

Graph to decide whether data is best modeled by a linear, quadratic, or exponential function.

Graph (–2, 0), (–1, –3), (0, –4), (1, –3), (2, 0). What kind of model best describes the data?

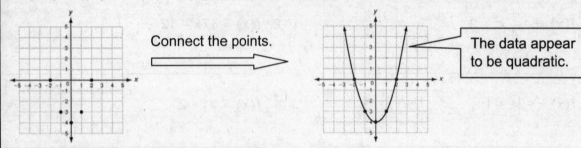

Connect the points.

The data appear to be quadratic.

You can also look at patterns in data to determine the correct model.

Linear functions have constant 1st differences.		**Quadratic functions have constant 2nd differences.**		**Exponential functions have a constant ratio.**	

x	y
2	5
4	2
6	–1
8	–4

–3
–3
–3

x	y
1	–8
2	–5
3	0
4	7

+3
+5   +2
+7   +2

x	y
0	–2
1	–8
2	–32
3	–128

×4
×4
×4

Graph each data set. Which kind of model best describes the data?

1. (–2, –4), (–1, –2), (0, 0), (1, 2), (2, 4)

2. (–1, 4), (0, 2), (1, 1), $\left(2, \frac{1}{2}\right)$, $\left(3, \frac{1}{4}\right)$

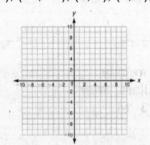

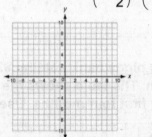

_____

_____

Look for a pattern in each data set to determine which kind of model best describes the data.

3.
x	y
0	6
1	12
2	24
3	48

4.
x	y
0	10
1	18
2	28
3	40

5.
x	y
3	4
6	–2
9	–8
12	–14

_____   _____   _____

LESSON
18-1
Piecewise Functions
Practice and Problem Solving: A/B

For each function, find $f(-2)$, $f(-1)$, $f(0)$, $f(1)$, and $f(2)$. Then graph the function.

1. $f(x) = \begin{cases} x - 1 & \text{if } x < 0 \\ x + 1 & \text{if } x \geq 0 \end{cases}$

2. $f(x) = \begin{cases} -3 & \text{if } x \leq 1 \\ -2x + 5 & \text{if } x > 1 \end{cases}$

_____   _____

_____   _____

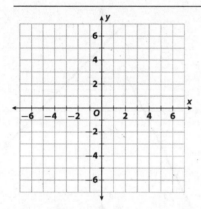   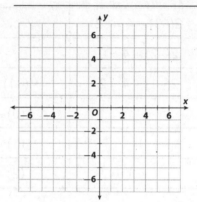

For each function, complete the table. Then graph the function.

3. $f(x) = [x] + 2$

x	2	3.5	−1.2	−0.7
f(x)				

4. $f(x) = 3[x]$

x	−1	−0.8	0.4	1.5
f(x)				

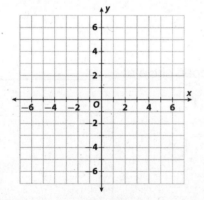   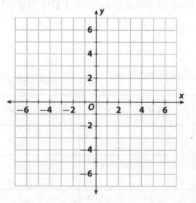

A consultant charges \$250 for the first four hours of work. She then charges \$50 per hour after four hours. Write an equation for each situation.

5. The consultant charges for parts of an hour after four hours of work.

_____

6. The consultant charges only for whole hours.

_____

LESSON 18-1

Piecewise Functions

Reteach

Use a table of values to graph a piecewise function.

Graph: $f(x) = \begin{cases} 2x+4 & \text{if } x < -1 \\ -x+3 & \text{if } x \geq -1 \end{cases}$

Evaluate both $2x + 4$ and $-x + 3$ at $x = -1$ to graph.

Make a table of values.

x	f(x) = 2x + 4	f(x) = -x + 3
-4	2(-4) + 4 = -4	
-3	2(-3) + 4 = -2	
-2	2(-2) + 4 = 0	
-1	2(-1) + 4 = 2	-(-1) + 3 = 4
0		-(0) + 3 = 3
1		-(1) + 3 = 2
2		-(2) + 3 = 1

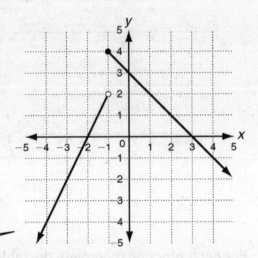

Check the split.
At $x = -1$, $f(x) = -x + 3$.
Put a closed circle at (-1, 4).
Put an open circle at (-1, 2).

Complete the table and graph the function.

1. $g(x) = \begin{cases} -2x & \text{if } x \leq 1 \\ x - 4 & \text{if } x > 1 \end{cases}$

Put a closed circle at _____. Put an open circle at _____ .

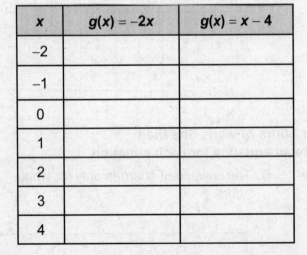

x	g(x) = -2x	g(x) = x - 4
-2		
-1		
0		
1		
2		
3		
4		

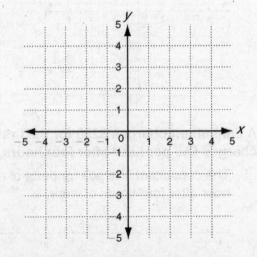

LESSON 18-2

Absolute Value Functions

Practice and Problem Solving: A/B

Graph each function. Then identify the vertex, domain, and range.

1. $f(x) = |x| + 2$

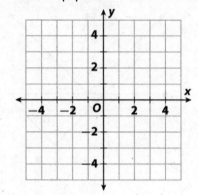

_____

2. $f(x) = -|x - 4|$

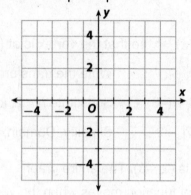

_____

3. $f(x) = -3|x| + 5$

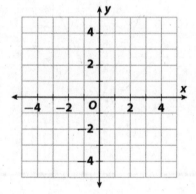

_____

4. $f(x) = |x + 1| - 1$

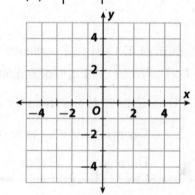

_____

Charles meets with customers on a daily basis. He uses the function $f(x) = 5|x - 8| + 20$ to calculate how many dollars he charges, per hour, for his time.

5. How much does Charles charge per hour if a customer hires him for 3 hours?

_____

_____

6. Find the lowest hourly rate that Charles charges. Show your work.

_____

_____

LESSON 18-2

Absolute Value Functions
Reteach

The graph of the absolute-value parent function is shaped like a V.

To **translate** $f(x) = |x|$ to a new **vertex** (h, k), use $g(x) = |x - h| + k$.

Example

Translate $f(x) = |x|$ so that the vertex is at $(2, -3)$.

$g(x) = |x - h| + k$ Write the transformation.

$g(x) = |x - 2| + (-3)$ Substitute $h = 2$, $k = -3$.

$g(x) = |x - 2| - 3$ Simplify. Domain: all x; Range: $y \geq -3$

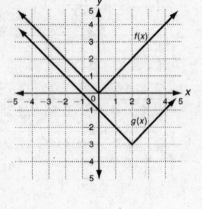

The vertex is $(2, -3)$. The entire graph
of the parent function moves when the vertex moves.

To **vertically** stretch or shrink $f(x)$ by a factor of a, use $f(x) \rightarrow a \cdot f(x)$.

To **horizontally** stretch or shrink $f(x)$ by a factor of b, use $f(x) \rightarrow f(\frac{1}{b}x)$.

Example

Stretch the graph of $f(x) = |x| + 1$ vertically by a factor of 2.

$g(x) \rightarrow a \cdot f(x)$ Write the transformation.

$g(x) = 2(|x| + 1)$ Substitute the factor of 2 for a.

$g(x) = 2|x| + 2$ Distribute. Vertex is at $(0, 2)$.

                  Domain: all x; Range: $y \geq 2$

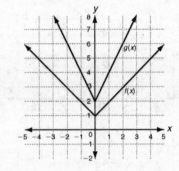

Graph each function. Identify the vertex, domain, and range.

1. $g(x) = |x - 1| + 2$

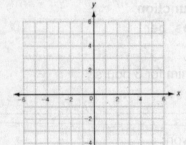

Vertex:_____

Domain:_____

Range:_____

2. $g(x) = |x + 3| - 1$

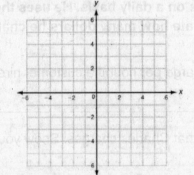

Vertex: _____

Domain: _____

Range: _____

3. $g(x) = 3|x| + 1$

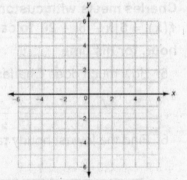

Vertex:_____

Domain:_____

Range:_____

LESSON 18-3 Transforming Absolute Value Functions

Practice and Problem Solving: A/B

State how you would transform the graph of the parent function
$f(x) = |x|$ **to graph** $g(x)$.

1. $g(x) = |x + 4| - 1$

   _____

2. $g(x) = 3|x - 3| + 7$

   _____

3. $g(x) = -5|x - 2| + 4$

   _____

4. $g(x) = -\frac{3}{4}|x + 12| + 12$

   _____

Sketch each function on the coordinate grid.

5. $f(x) = -2|x - 2| + 3$

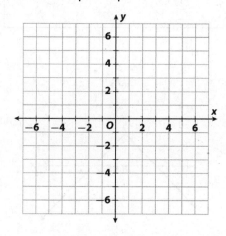

6. $f(x) = \frac{2}{3}|x + 1| - 5$

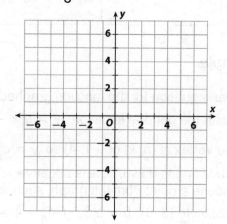

Write a function rule for each graph shown.

7.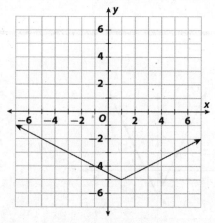

   _____

8.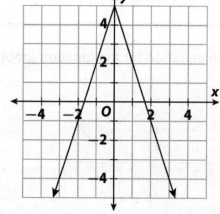

   _____

LESSON 18-3

Transforming Absolute Value Functions

Reteach

Transform the graph of the absolute value function, $y = a|x - h| + k$, by changing the values of a, h, and k.

A change to this value	has this effect on the graph	Example
k $y = a\|x - h\| + \boldsymbol{k}$	moves up (+) or down (−)	$k = -4$ $y = \|x\| - 4$ shifts vertex down 4
h $y = a\|x - \boldsymbol{h}\| + k$	moves left (−) or right (+)	$h = 4$ $y = \|x - 4\|$ shifts vertex right 4
a $y = \boldsymbol{a}\|x - h\| + k$	spreads ($0 < \|a\| < 1$) or shrinks ($\|a\| > 1$) the V When $a < 0$, the V opens down.	$y = 2.5\|x\|$ shrinks the V $y = 0.5\|x\|$ spreads the V $y = -\|x\|$ reflects the V

Example

Write an equation for the function graphed.

Start with the general equation: $y = a|x - h| + k$

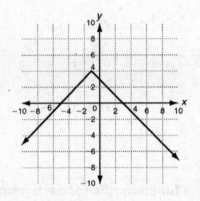

The vertex is (h, k) or $(-1, 4)$ so $y = a|x - (-1)| + 4$.

The V opens down, so a is negative.
Choose a point from the graph, such as $(3, 0)$.

Substitute $(3, 0)$: $0 = a|3 - (-1)| + 4$ and solve for a.

$0 = a|3 - (-1)| + 4$ so $a = -1$.

The equation is $y = -1|x + 1| + 4$.

Write an equation for the function graphed.

1.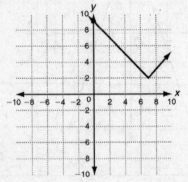

_____

2.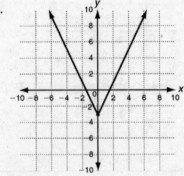

_____

Name _____ Date _____ Class_____

Solving Absolute-Value Equations and Inequalities
Practice and Problem Solving: A/B

Solve each equation.

1. $|x| = 12$

    _____

2. $|x| = \dfrac{1}{2}$

    _____

3. $|x| - 6 = 4$

    _____

4. $5 + |x| = 14$

    _____

5. $3|x| = 24$

    _____

6. $|x + 3| = 10$

    _____

7. $|x - 1| = 2$

    _____

8. $4|x - 5| = 12$

    _____

9. $|x + 2| - 3 = 9$

    _____

10. $|6x| = 18$

    _____

11. $|x - 1| = 0$

    _____

12. $|x - 3| + 2 = 2$

    _____

13. How many solutions does the equation $|x + 7| = 1$ have? _____

14. How many solutions does the equation $|x + 7| = 0$ have? _____

15. How many solutions does the equation $|x + 7| = -1$ have? _____

Leticia sets the thermostat in her apartment to 68 degrees. The actual temperature in her apartment can vary from this by as much as 3.5 degrees.

16. Write an absolute-value equation that you can

    use to find the minimum and maximum temperature. _____

17. Solve the equation to find the minimum and

    maximum temperature. _____

Solve each inequality. Then graph the solution.

18. $|9x| \geq 18$

19. $|3x - 7| > 8$

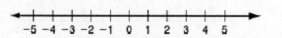

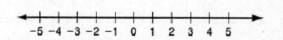

LESSON 18-4

Solving Absolute-Value Equations and Inequalities
Reteach

There are three steps in solving an absolute-value equation.

Solve $|x - 3| + 4 = 8$.

> **Step 1:** Isolate the absolute-value expression.
>
> $|x - 3| + 4 = 8$
>
> $\underline{\quad\quad -4 \quad -4\quad}$ *Subtract 4 from both sides.*
>
> $|x - 3| = 4$
>
> **Step 2:** Rewrite the equation as two cases.
>
> $$|x - 3| = 4$$
>
>
>
>   **Case 1**   **Case 2**
>
> **Step 3:** $x - 3 = -4$ $x - 3 = 4$
>
> Solve. $\underline{\;+3\quad +3\;}$ $\underline{\;+3\quad +3\;}$ *Add 3 to both sides.*
>
> $x = -1$ $x = 7$
>
> The solutions are -1 and 7.

Solve each equation.

1. $|x - 2| - 3 = 5$

2. $|x + 7| + 2 = 10$

3. $4|x - 5| = 20$

4. $|2x| + 1 = 7$

LESSON 19-1 Square Root Functions

Practice and Problem Solving: A/B

Find the domain of each function.

1. $y = \sqrt{x - 6}$

_____

2. $y = -\sqrt{x + 1} - 4$

_____

3. $y = \frac{1}{2}\sqrt{3x - 2}$

_____

4. $y = \sqrt{4(x + 5)}$

_____

5. $y = 10 - \sqrt{5x + 3}$

_____

6. $y = \sqrt{1 - x}$

_____

Graph the function $f(x)$ for the domain $x \geq 0$. Then graph its inverse, $f^{-1}(x)$, and write a rule for the inverse function.

7. $f(x) = \frac{1}{4}x^2$

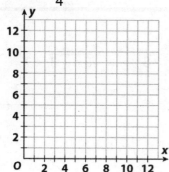

8. $f(x) = -\frac{1}{3}x^2$

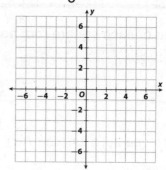

_____

The function $d = 4.9t^2$ gives the distance, d, in meters, that an object dropped from a height will fall in t seconds. Use this for Problems 9–10.

9. Express t as a function of d.

_____

10. Find the number of seconds it takes an object to fall 100 feet. Round to the nearest tenth of a second.

_____

LESSON 19-1

Square Root Functions

Reteach

The graph of the parent square root function, $g(x) = \sqrt{x}$ looks like this:

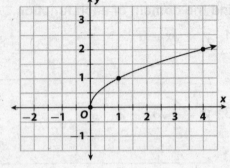

The function $g(x) = \sqrt{x}$ is the inverse of

$f(x) = x^2$ for $x \geq 0$

Notice that the graph is in Quadrant I only.

The domain is $x \geq 0$.
This is because $g(x) = \sqrt{x}$ is not defined for real numbers if $x < 0$.

Example

Find the domain of $y = \sqrt{2x + 1} + 5$.

$2x + 1 \geq 0$ Look at possible values for what is under the square root sign.
$x \geq -\frac{1}{2}$ Solve the inequality.

The domain is the set of all real numbers greater than or equal to $-\frac{1}{2}$.

Find the domain of each square root equation.

1. $y = \sqrt{x - 1} - 2$

2. $y = \sqrt{3x + 2} + 3$

3. $y = \sqrt{2x - 3} + 7$

_____   _____   _____

The inverse of a quadratic function $f(x) = ax^2$ for $x \geq 0$ is $f^{-1}(x) = \sqrt{\frac{x}{a}}$, $a \neq 0$.

Example

$f(x) = -2x^2$ for $x \geq 0$ Write a rule for the inverse function $f^{-1}(x)$.

$f(x) = -2x^2$ $a = -2$

$f^{-1}(x) = \sqrt{\frac{x}{-2}}$ Substitute the value for a in $f^{-1}(x) = \sqrt{\frac{x}{a}}$.

In order for $\frac{x}{-2}$ to be non-negative, $\frac{x}{-2} \geq 0$. Solving for x REVERSES the inquality sign

since you are multiplying by a negative number (-2). The solution is $x \leq 0$.

$f^{-1}(x) = \sqrt{\frac{x}{-2}}$ for $x \leq 0$.

Write a rule for the inverse function. Include the restrictions on x.

4. $f(x) = 3x^2$

5. $f(x) = \frac{1}{2}x^2$

6. $f(x) = -5x^2$

_____   _____   _____

LESSON
19-2
Transforming Square Root Functions
Practice and Problem Solving: A/B

Find the domain and range of each function.

1. $y = 0.4\sqrt{x + 3} - 7$

2. $y = 3 + 8\sqrt{x - 1}$

_____

3. $y = -6 + \dfrac{2}{3}\sqrt{x - 5}$

_____

4. $y = 10\sqrt{x - 9}$

_____

Graph each square root function. Then describe the graph as a transformation of the graph of the parent function, and give its domain and range.

5. $y = 3\sqrt{x + 4} + 2$

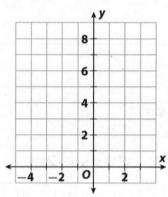

6. $y = \dfrac{1}{2}\sqrt{x - 2} + 3$

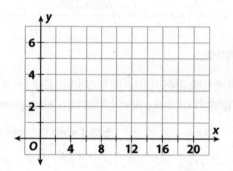

_____

_____

Solve.

7. To graph the function $f(x)$, the parent function $y = \sqrt{x}$ is stretched vertically by a factor of 4 and translated 3 units to the right. Write a possible function rule for $f(x)$.

_____

8. Does the function $f(x) = 2\sqrt{x - 1} + 10$ have a minimum value or a maximum value? If so, find it. If not, explain why not.

_____

LESSON
19-2
Transforming Square Root Functions
Reteach

Transform the graph of the square root function, $y = a\sqrt{x-h} + k$, by changing the values of a, h, and k. The point (h, k) is the endpoint of the graph.

A change to this value	has this effect on the graph	Example
k $y = a\sqrt{x-h} + \boldsymbol{k}$	moves up (+) or down (−)	$k = -4$ $y = \sqrt{x} - 4$ shifts the endpoint down 4
h $y = a\sqrt{x-\boldsymbol{h}} + k$	moves left (−) or right (+)	$h = 4$ $y = \sqrt{x-4}$ shifts the endpoint right 4
a $y = \boldsymbol{a}\sqrt{x-h} + k$	$(0 < \lvert a \rvert < 1)$ is a vertical shrink of the graph. $(\lvert a \rvert > 1)$ is a vertical stretch of the graph. When $a < 0$, the graph is reflected.	$y = 0.5\sqrt{x}$ vertical shrink $y = 2.5\sqrt{x}$ vertical stretch $y = -\sqrt{x}$ reflection

Example

Describe the graph of the function $g(x) = \sqrt{x+2}$ as a transformation of the graph of the parent function and give the domain and range.

$f(x) = \sqrt{x}$

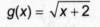

Start with the general equation:
$$y = a\sqrt{x-h} + k$$

The value of a is unchanged. $a = 1$

$h = -2$ which shifts the endpoint left 2.

The value of k is unchanged. $k = 0$

Domain: $x \geq -2$; Range: $x \geq 0$

$g(x) = \sqrt{x+2}$

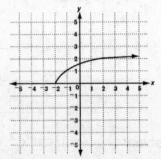

Describe the graph of each function as a transformation of the graph of the parent function and give the domain and range.

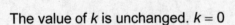

1. $g(x) = \sqrt{x-1} - 3$

2. $g(x) = -\sqrt{x} + 5$

_____

_____

_____

Name _____ Date _____ Class_____

LESSON 19-3 **Cube Root Functions**

Practice and Problem Solving: A/B

Find the inverse of each cubic function.

1. $f(x) = x^3$

2. $f(x) = \frac{1}{8}x^3$

_____

_____

3. $f(x) = -27x^3$

4. $f(x) = 5x^3$

_____

_____

5. $f(x) = 125x^3 - 7$

6. $f(x) = x^3 + 8$

_____

_____

Graph the function $f(x)$. Then graph its inverse, $f^{-1}(x)$, and write a rule for the inverse function.

7. $f(x) = \frac{1}{2}x^3$

8. $f(x) = -3x^3$

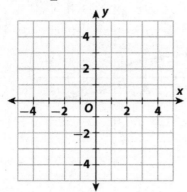

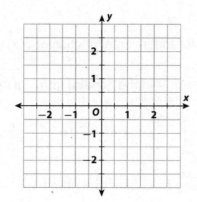

In a square cylinder, height, h, equals diameter, d. The function

$V = \frac{\pi}{4}d^3$ **gives the volume, V, of a square cylinder. Use this for Problems 9–10.**

9. Express d as a function of V.

_____

10. Find the diameter of a square cylinder of volume 300 cubic inches. Round to the nearest tenth of an inch.

_____

**LESSON
19-3**

Cube Root Functions

Reteach

The graph of the parent cubic function, $f(x) = x^3$ looks like this:

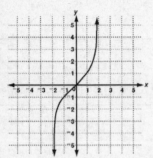

The function $g(x) = \sqrt[3]{x}$ is the inverse of $f(x) = x^3$.
The graph $g(x) = \sqrt[3]{x}$ looks like this:

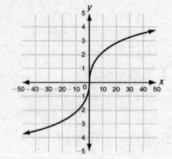

For both $f(x) = x^3$ and $g(x) = \sqrt[3]{x}$, the domain and range are both the set of real numbers.

The inverse of the function $f(x) = ax^3$ is the function $g(x) = \sqrt[3]{\dfrac{x}{a}}$.

The inverse of the function $f(x) = -x^3$ is the function $g(x) = \sqrt[3]{-x}$.

Example

Write a rule for the inverse function of $f(x) = -\dfrac{3}{2}x^3$.

Substitute $a = \dfrac{-3}{2}$ in the general form: $g(x) = \sqrt[3]{\dfrac{x}{-\frac{3}{2}}}$

Simplify: $x \div \left(-\dfrac{3}{2}\right) = x \bullet \left(-\dfrac{2}{3}\right) = \dfrac{-2x}{3}$ So, $g(x) = \sqrt[3]{-\dfrac{2}{3}x}$.

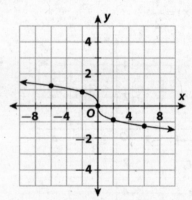

Use a graphing calculator and graph $y = \left(-\left(\dfrac{2}{3}\right)x\right)^{\left(\frac{1}{3}\right)}$.

Write a rule for the inverse of each function and sketch the graph.

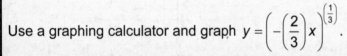

1. $f(x) = -3x^3$

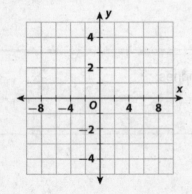

2. $f(x) = \dfrac{1}{2}x^3$

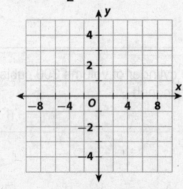

3. $f(x) = -\dfrac{2}{5}x^3$

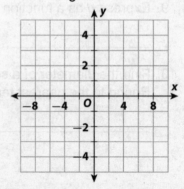

Name _____ Date _____ Class_____

LESSON
19-4
Transforming Cube Root Functions
Practice and Problem Solving: A/B

Graph each cube root function. Then describe the graph as a transformation of the graph of the parent function. (The graph of the parent function is shown.)

1. $g(x) = \sqrt[3]{x+2} - 3$

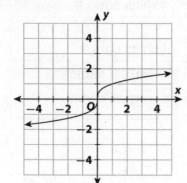

2. $g(x) = 2\sqrt[3]{x-3} + 2$

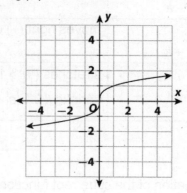

_____   _____

Write the equation of the cube root function whose graph is shown.

3.

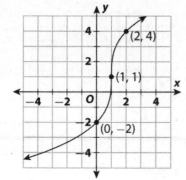

4.

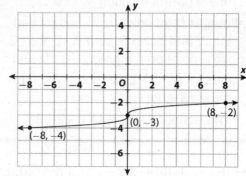

_____   _____

Solve.

5. The graph of $y = \sqrt[3]{x}$ is reflected across the x-axis. The graph is then translated 11 units up and 7 units to the left. Write the equation of the final graph.

_____

6. The graph of $y = \sqrt[3]{x}$ is stretched vertically by a factor of 6. The graph is then translated 9 units to the right and 3 units down. Write the equation of the final graph.

_____

LESSON 19-4

Transforming Cube Root Functions
Reteach

Transform the graph of the parent cube root function by changing the values of *a*, *h*, and *k* in $y = a\sqrt[3]{x - h} + k$.

A change to this value	has this effect on the graph	Example
k $y = a\sqrt[3]{x - h} + \mathbf{k}$	moves up (+) or down (−)	$k = -4$ $y = \sqrt[3]{x} - 4$ shifts down 4
h $y = a\sqrt[3]{x - \mathbf{h}} + k$	moves right (+) or left (−)	$h = 4$ $y = \sqrt[3]{x - 4}$ shifts right 4
a $y = \mathbf{a}\sqrt[3]{x - h} + k$	stretches ($|a| > 1$) or shrinks ($0 < |a| < 1$)	$y = 2.5\sqrt[3]{x}$ vertical stretch $y = 0.5\sqrt[3]{x}$ vertical shrink

Example

Write the equation of the cube root function whose graph is shown.

Start with the general equation: $y = a\sqrt[3]{x - h} + k$

The point (0, 0) is the center of the graph
    of the parent function $y = \sqrt[3]{x}$.

That center point point (*h*, *k*) has moved
    left 2, and down 3, so $h = -2$, $k = -3$.

Choose a point on the graph (−1, 1) and substitute
    into $1 = a\sqrt[3]{-1 + 2} - 3$ and solve for *a*.
    $1 = a - 3$ so $a = 4$
    The equation is $y = 4\sqrt[3]{x + 2} - 3$.

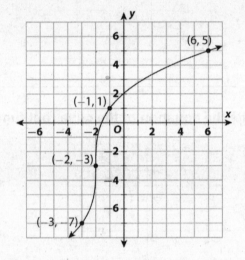

Write the equation of the cube root function whose graph is shown.

1.

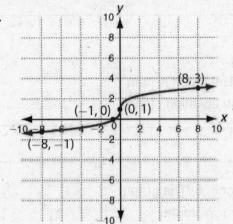

2.

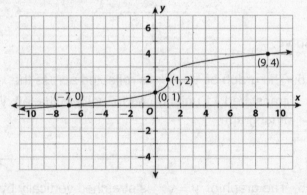

_____

_____

LESSON
A-1

The Pythagorean Theorem

Practice and Problem Solving: A/B

Find the missing side to the nearest tenth.

1.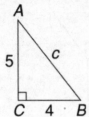

_____

2.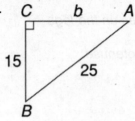

_____

3.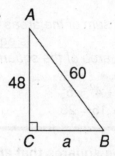

_____

4.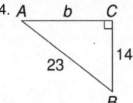

_____

5.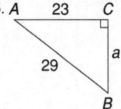

_____

6.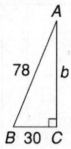

_____

Solve.

7. Jane and Miguel are siblings. They go to different schools. Jane walks 6 blocks east from home. Miguel walks 8 blocks north. How many blocks apart would the two schools be if you could walk straight from one school to the other?

_____

8. The base of a rectangular box has a width of 3 inches and a length of 4 inches. The box is 12 inches tall.

   a. Draw a picture of the box below.

   b. How far is it from one of the box's top corners to the opposite corner of the base of the box?

_____

LESSON
A-1

The Pythagorean Theorem
Reteach

In a **right triangle,**

    the sum of the areas of the squares on the legs
                   <u>is equal to</u>
    the area of the square on the hypotenuse.

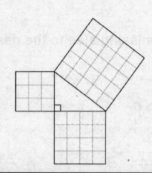

$$3^2 + 4^2 = 5^2$$
$$9 + 16 = 25$$

Given the squares that are on the legs of a right triangle, draw the square for the hypotenuse below or on another sheet of paper.

1. leg   leg   hypotenuse

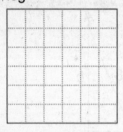 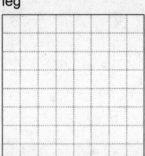

Without drawing the squares, you can find a missing leg or the hypotenuse when given the other sides.

Model   **Example 1**   **Example 2**

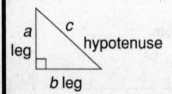   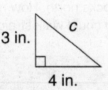   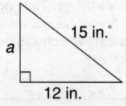

                        Solution 1   **Solution 2**

                        $a^2 + b^2 = c^2$ $a^2 + b^2 = c^2$
                        $3^2 + 4^2 = c^2$ $a^2 + 12^2 = 15^2$
                        $9 + 16 = c^2$ $a^2 = 225 - 144$
                        $25 = c^2$, so $c = 5$ in. $a^2 = 81$, so $a = 9$ in.

Find the missing side.

2.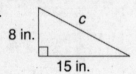

3.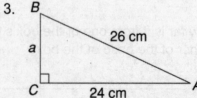

_____   _____

LESSON A-2

Converse of the Pythagorean Theorem

Practice and Problem Solving: A/B

Write "yes" for sides that form right triangles and "no" for sides that do not form right triangles. Prove that each answer is correct.

1. 7, 24, 25

2. 30, 40, 45

3. 21.6, 28.8, 36

_____

_____

_____

_____

_____

_____

4. 10, 15, 18

5. 10.5, 36, 50

6. 2.5, 6, 6.5

_____

_____

_____

_____

_____

_____

Solve.

7. A commuter airline files a new route between two cities that are 400 kilometers apart. One of the two cities is 200 kilometers from a third city. The other one of the two cities is 300 kilometers from the third city. Do the paths between the three cities form a right triangle? Prove that your answer is correct.

_____

_____

8. A school wants to build a rectangular playground that will have a diagonal length of 75 yards. How wide can the playground be if the length has to be 30 yards?

_____

9. A 250-foot length of fence is placed around a three-sided animal pen. Two of the sides of the pen are 100 feet long each. Does the fence form a right triangle? Prove that your answer is correct.

_____

_____

Converse of the Pythagorean Theorem
Reteach

LESSON A-2

Step 1 The first step in verifying that a triangle is a right triangle is to name the three sides. One side is the hypotenuse and the other two sides are legs.

- In a right triangle, the hypotenuse is opposite the right angle.

  ⟶   The hypotenuse is 5 cm.

- The hypotenuse is greater than either leg.

  ⟶   5 cm > 4 cm and 5 cm > 3 cm

Step 2 Next, the lengths of the hypotenuse and legs must satisfy the Pythagorean Theorem.

$$(\text{hypotenuse})^2 = (\text{first leg})^2 + (\text{second leg})^2$$

In the example above, $5^2 = 3^2 + 4^2 = 25$, so the triangle is a right triangle.

Conclusion If the lengths of the hypotenuse and the two legs satisfy the conditions of the Pythagorean Theorem, then the triangle is a right triangle. If they do not satisfy the conditions of the Pythagorean Theorem, the triangle is not a right triangle.

Find the length of each hypotenuse.

1.

_____

2.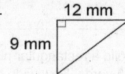

_____

First, fill in the length of the hypotenuse in each problem. Then, determine if the sides form a right triangle.

3. 1, 2, 3

Hypotenuse: _____

_____

4. 8, 7, 6

Hypotenuse: _____

_____

5. 15, 20, 25

Hypotenuse: _____

_____

Show that these sides form a right triangle.

6. 2, 3, $\sqrt{13}$

_____

7. 3, 6, $3\sqrt{5}$

_____

LESSON
A-3

Distance Between Two Points

Practice and Problem Solving: A/B

Name the coordinates of the points.

1.

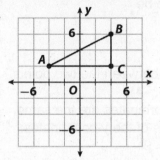

A(_____ , _____)

B(_____ , _____)

C(_____ , _____)

2.

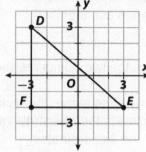

D(_____ , _____)

E(_____ , _____)

F(_____ , _____)

Name the hypotenuse of each right triangle in problems 1 and 2.

3. Hypotenuse in problem 1:   4. Hypotenuse in problem 2:

_____   _____

Estimate the length of the hypotenuse for each right triangle in problems 1 and 2.

5. Hypotenuse in problem 1:   6. Hypotenuse in problem 2:

_____   _____

Use the distance formula to calculate the length of the hypotenuse for each right triangle.

7. Hypotenuse in problem 1:   8. Hypotenuse in problem 2:

_____   _____

9. Use the distance formula to find the distance between the points
   (−4, −4) and (4, 4).

_____

LESSON A-3

Distance Between Two Points

Reteach

There are three cases of distance between two points on a coordinate plane. The first two have fewer steps than the third, but you have to be able to identify when to use them.

Case 1

The *x*-coordinates of the two points are the same.
If the *x*-coordinates are the same, the distance between the two points is the **absolute value** of the *difference* of the *y*-coordinates.
The line connecting the two points is a *vertical* line.

Example 1

Find the distance between the two points $A(-3, 5)$ and $B(-3, -4)$.
⟶ The *x*-coordinates are the same.
⟶ Difference of the *y*-coordinates:
$5 - (-4) = 9$
⟶ The absolute value of 9 is 9.

Case 2

The *y*-coordinates of the two points are the same.
If the *y*-coordinates are the same, the distance between the two points is the **absolute value** of the *difference* of the *x*-coordinates.
The line connecting the two points is a *horizontal* line.

Example 2

Find the distance between the two points $C(1, 3)$ and $D(6, 3)$.
⟶ The *y*-coordinates are the same.
⟶ Difference of the *x*-coordinates:
$1 - 6 = -5$
⟶ The absolute value of −5 is 5.

Case 3

If the *x* and *y*-coordinates of the two points are different, use the distance formula:
$$d = \sqrt{(x_2 - x_1)^2 + (y_2 - y_1)^2}$$
The *x* and *y*-coordinates are different if $x_1 \neq x_2$ and $y_1 \neq y_2$.
The line connecting the two points can be thought of as the *hypotenuse* of a right triangle.

Example 3

Find the distance between the two points $E(-9, 5)$ and $F(-4, 0)$.
⟶ Use the distance formula.
⟶ $d = \sqrt{(-4+9)^2 + (0-5)^2}$
$= \sqrt{5^2 + (-5)^2} = 5\sqrt{2}$

Tell whether the points given are endpoints of a vertical line, a horizontal line, or neither.

1. $(-8, 1), (-5, 1)$ 2. $(4, 3), (2, 1)$ 3. $(0, 0), (0, 100)$ 4. $(3, 3), (3, 3)$

_____   _____   _____   _____

Use the distance formula to find the distance between the two points.

5. $(0.5, 1.3), (-0.4, -1.2)$ 6. $(6, -3), (2, -4)$